SCHOLASTIC

Now I Know My

NUMBERS, COLORS, SHAPES & MORE

New York • Toronto • London • Auckland • Sydney **Teaching** *Resources*
Mexico City • New Delhi • Hong Kong • Buenos Aires

No part of this publication may be reproduced in whole or in part, or stored in a retrieval system, or transmitted in any form or by any means, electronic, photocopying, recording, or otherwise, without written permission of the publisher. For information regarding permission, write to Scholastic Inc., 557 Broadway, New York, NY 10012-3999.

Edited by Immacula A. Rhodes
Cover design by Lindsey Dekker
Cover art by Mike Dammer
Interior design by Holly Grundon

ISBN: 978-0-545-77682-0
Written and illustrated by Lucia Kemp Henry

Copyright © 2014 by Scholastic Inc.
All rights reserved.
Published by Scholastic Inc.
Printed in the U.S.A.

2 3 4 5 6 7 8 9 10   40   21 30 19 18 17 16

Contents

NUMBERS

Now I Know My Numbers, Colors, Shapes & More © 2014 Scholastic Teaching Resources

PATTERNS

Now I Know My Numbers, Colors, Shapes & More © 2014 Scholastic Teaching Resources

Introduction

Welcome to *Now I Know My Numbers, Colors, Shapes & More*! This big collection of activity pages will give your child plenty of opportunities to practice and master key early concepts and develop fine-motor skills. Best of all, your child will experience the joy of learning while building skills that will help him or her excel in school and become a lifelong learner.

Research shows that independent practice helps children gain mastery of essential skills. Each double-sided activity page targets specific skills and concepts for your child to practice. The consistent format will help your child work independently and with confidence. Other important features include:

* easy-to-follow directions to help build vocabulary and early reading comprehension skills

* tracing, drawing, and writing exercises to develop and strengthen your child's fine-motor skills

* appealing artwork that engages and motivates your child to learn

The activity pages provide focused practice in the following skills and concepts:

Numbers

* Identifying and writing numbers and number words

* Counting to 100

* Distinguishing between odd and even numbers

* Comparing sets

Colors, Shapes & Patterns

* Identifying different colors and shapes

* Reading and writing words for colors and shapes

* Tracing, drawing, and matching shapes

* Recognizing and creating basic patterns

On the next page, you'll find suggestions for introducing the activity pages to your child along with tips for making the experience go smoothly. Pages 9–14 provide a close-up look at the various activity formats, and for your reference, page 15 details how the activity pages will help your child meet key early math, reading, and language curriculum standards.

We hope you enjoy doing the activities in this book with your child. Your involvement will help make this a valuable educational experience and will support and enhance your child's learning!

Getting Started

Each activity consists of a double-sided page that offers practice in a specific skill or concept. Introduce the activity to your child by going over the directions and walking through its features. See pages 9–14 for more information.

Helpful Tips

❖ For ease of use, simply choose the skill(s) or concept(s) you would like your child to work on (you'll find detailed information on the Contents pages), locate the corresponding activity page in the book, and gently tear out the page along the perforated edges.

❖ The only materials needed for the activities are crayons or colored pencils.

❖ Let your child complete each page at his or her own pace.

❖ Review the answers together and encourage your child to share the thinking behind his or her responses.

❖ Support your child's efforts and offer help when needed.

❖ Display your child's work and share his or her progress with family and friends!

A Close-Up Look at the Activity Pages

You'll find several activity formats that repeat throughout the book, as described below:

NUMBERS

❖ **Trace the Number:** Your child traces the number and then writes it without guides. This exercise reinforces number formation and helps build fine-motor skills.

❖ **Identify the Number:** Visual discrimination skills are reinforced as your child distinguishes the target number from an array of other numbers.

❖ **Hidden Picture:** Your child identifies the target number and colors that space as directed to reveal a hidden picture or shape.

❖ **Count and Color:** Counting skills get a boost as your child counts out and colors a specific number of items.

❖ **Drawing:** This activity develops fine-motor skills while reinforcing the target number.

❖ **Count the Sets:** Your child makes the connection between quantities and numbers in print by counting and writing the number of items in sets.

* **Trace the Word:** This activity reinforces word recognition, spelling, and letter formation as your child traces the number word and then writes it without guides.

* **Identify the Word:** Your child uses visual discrimination skills to identify the target number word from similarly spelled or shaped words.

* **Color the Quantity:** Coloring the specified number of items helps reinforce counting skills.

* **Connect-the-Dot Puzzle:** Your child builds skills in counting to higher numbers (from 30 to 100) with these simple connect-the-dot activities.

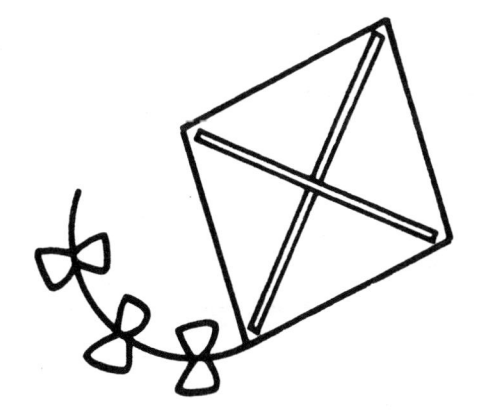

❖ **Odd or Even Number:** Your child fills in the missing numbers and then colors all of the odd or even numbers in the series.

❖ **Compare Sets:** In this activity, your child compares two sets to determine which has more or fewer items.

❖ **Match Numbers and Words:** Your child draws lines to match each number to the correct number word.

❖ **Number Chart:** As your child writes numbers in the chart, he or she practices sequencing and number formation.

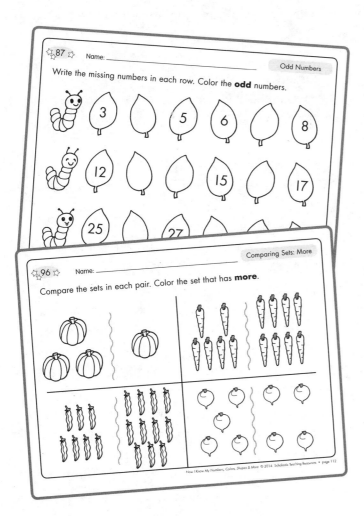

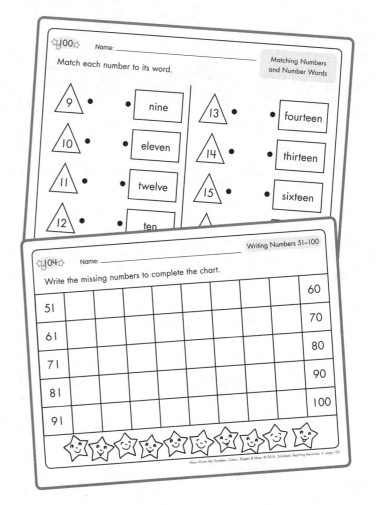

COLORS

❖ **Trace and Write:** Your child traces a specific color word and then writes the word without guides. This exercise reinforces letter formation, word recognition, and spelling.

❖ **Identify Object Colors:** In this activity, your child identifies and colors objects that are commonly found—in real life—in a specific color.

❖ **Identify the Word:** Your child uses visual discrimination skills to identify the target color word from similarly spelled or shaped words.

❖ **Drawing:** This activity helps develop fine-motor skills while reinforcing the target color concept.

❖ **Fill-in-the-Blank:** Your child uses context clues to write the target color word in a sentence that connects to the picture he or she drew in the previous activity.

❖ **Review:** Color-coded pictures help reinforce color-word recognition and fine-motor skills. A writing activity offers additional practice in recognizing, spelling, and writing color words.

❖ **Color Patterns:** Your child uses a color key to create AB, AAB, ABB, AABB, and ABC patterns.

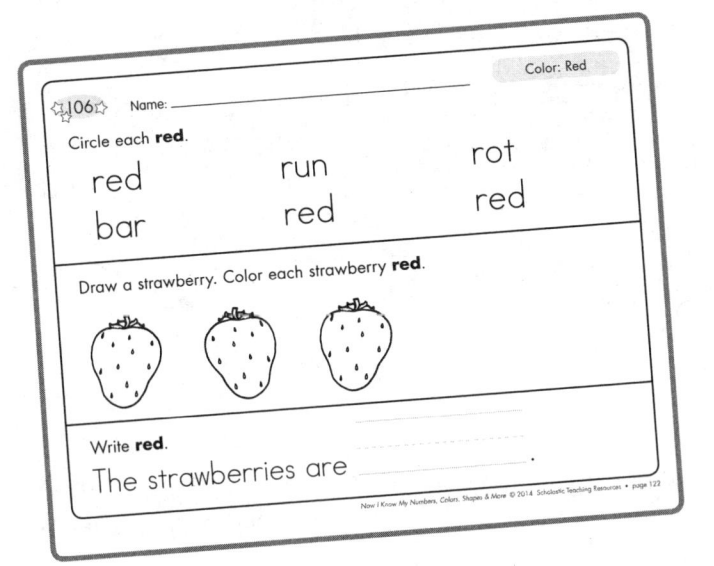

SHAPES

✤ **Trace the Shape:** To develop shape recognition and fine-motor skills, your child traces a specific shape in two sections of these activity pages.

✤ **Identify the Shape:** Your child identifies the target shape from a variety of shapes and then colors the appropriate ones.

✤ **Trace and Write:** In this activity, your child traces the target shape word and then writes the word without guides.

✤ **Drawing:** To build understanding of shape concepts and fine-motor skills, your child draws a picture using a specific shape.

✤ **Review:** These color-coded pictures reinforce shape-word recognition and fine-motor skills. A writing activity gives your child more practice in recognizing, spelling, and writing shape words.

✤ **Shape Patterns:** Your child draws shapes to complete AB, AAB, ABB, AABB, and ABC patterns.

✤ **Identify Attributes:** The activities on these pages help sharpen reasoning skills. Your child colors the shapes and then identifies which shape matches the specific attributes stated in the directions.

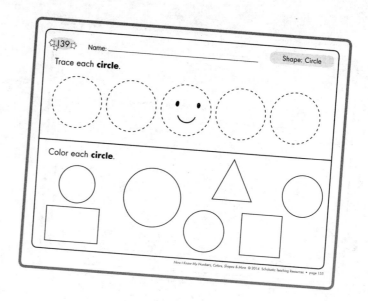

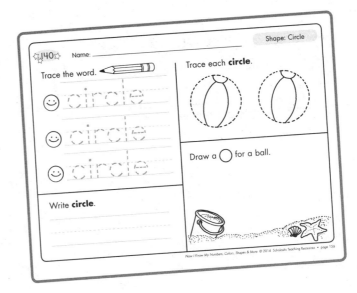

PATTERNS

❖ **Complete the Patterns:** Your child completes patterns by drawing pictures or filling in the missing letter or numbers. Each activity page features a variety of patterns.

❖ **Review:** In these activities, your child demonstrates understanding of patterns by identifying the item or shape that comes next in a pattern, as well as by creating patterns.

❖ **Identify Patterns:** Your child identifies, labels, and creates AB, AAB, ABB, AABB, and ABC patterns.

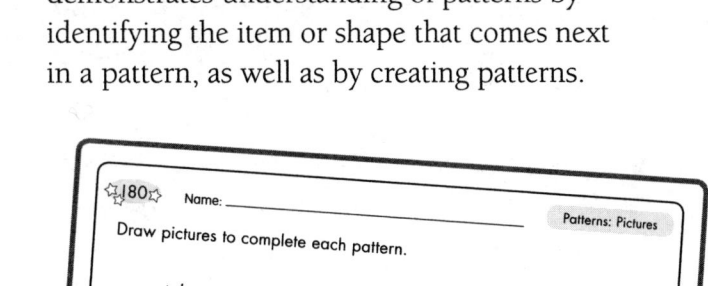

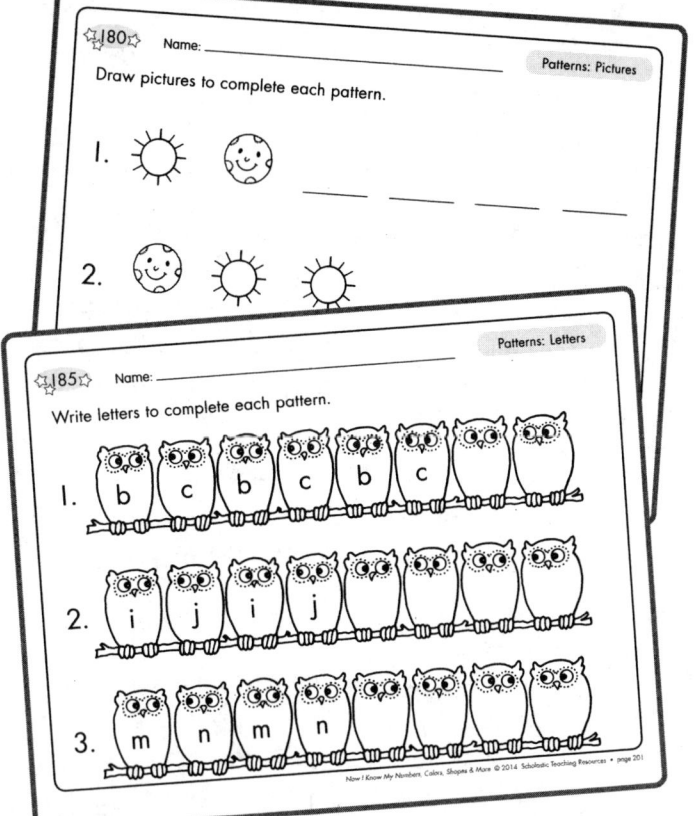

Connections to the Standards

The activities in this book support the College and Career Readiness (CCR) Standards. These broad standards, which serve as the basis of many state standards, were developed to establish grade-by-grade educational expectations with the goal of providing students nationwide with a quality education that prepares them for college and careers. The standards begin in kindergarten, so, if your child is of preschool age, the activities will help set the stage for your child's success with the following early mathematics, reading, and language standards for students in kindergarten and first grade.

MATHEMATICS

Counting and Cardinality

- Know number names and the count sequence.
- Count to 100 by ones and by tens.
- Count forward beginning from a given number within the known sequence.
- Write numbers from 0 to 20. Represent a number of objects with a written numeral, 0–20.
- Understand the relationship between numbers and quantities; connect counting to cardinality.
- Count to answer "how many?" questions; given a number from 1–20, count out that many objects.
- Identify whether the number of objects in one group is greater than, less than, or equal to the number of objects in another group.
- Compare two numbers between 1 and 10 presented as written numerals.

Geometry

- Correctly name shapes regardless of their orientations or overall size.
- Analyze and compare two-dimensional shapes, in different sizes and orientations.
- Distinguish between defining attributes (e.g., triangles are closed and three-sided) and non-defining attributes (e.g., color, orientation, overall sizes).

READING

Print Concepts

Demonstrate understanding of the organization and basic features of print.

- Follow words from left to right and top to bottom.
- Recognize that spoken words are represented in written language by specific sequences of letters.
- Understand that words are separated by spaces in print.
- Recognize and name all upper- and lowercase letters of the alphabet.
- Recognize the distinguishing features of a sentence (e.g., first word, capitalization, ending punctuation).

Phonological Awareness

- Demonstrate understanding of spoken words, syllables, and sounds.

Phonics and Word Recognition

- Know and apply grade-level phonics and word analysis skills in decoding words.

Fluency

- Read with sufficient accuracy and fluency to support comprehension.
- Read grade-level text with purpose and understanding.
- Use context to confirm or self-correct word recognition and understanding, rereading as necessary.

LANGUAGE

Conventions of Standard English

Demonstrate command of the conventions of standard English grammar and spelling when writing or speaking.

- Print upper- and lowercase letters.

© Copyright 2010. National Governors Association Center for Best Practices and Council of Chief State School Officers. All rights reserved.

Name: _____

one

Trace. Write.

Circle each **1**.

2 3 0 1

3 2 0

1 3 1

Find each **1**. Color that space yellow.
Then color the rest of the picture.

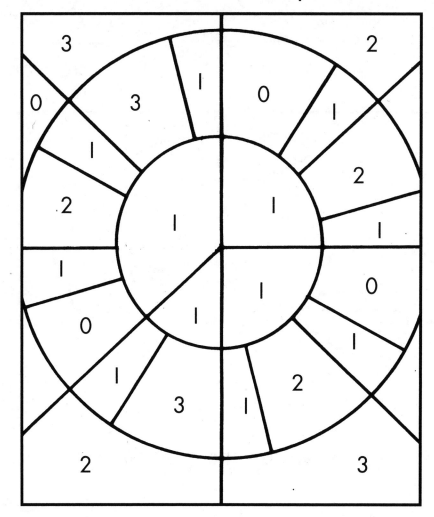

Name: _____

Color **1** sun in each row.

1.

2.

3.

Draw **1** sun in the sky.

How many suns? Write the number in the box.

Name: _____

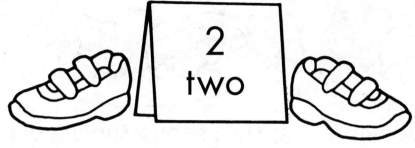

2
two

Trace. Write.

Circle each **2**.

2   I   2   0   3

0   3   I   2

Find each **2**. Color that space brown. Then color the rest of the picture.

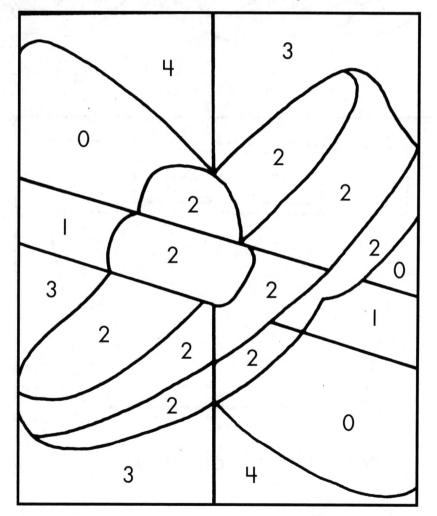

4 Name: _____

Color **2** shoes in each row.

1.

2.

3.

Draw **2** shoes in the box.

Shoes

How many shoes? Write the number in the circle.

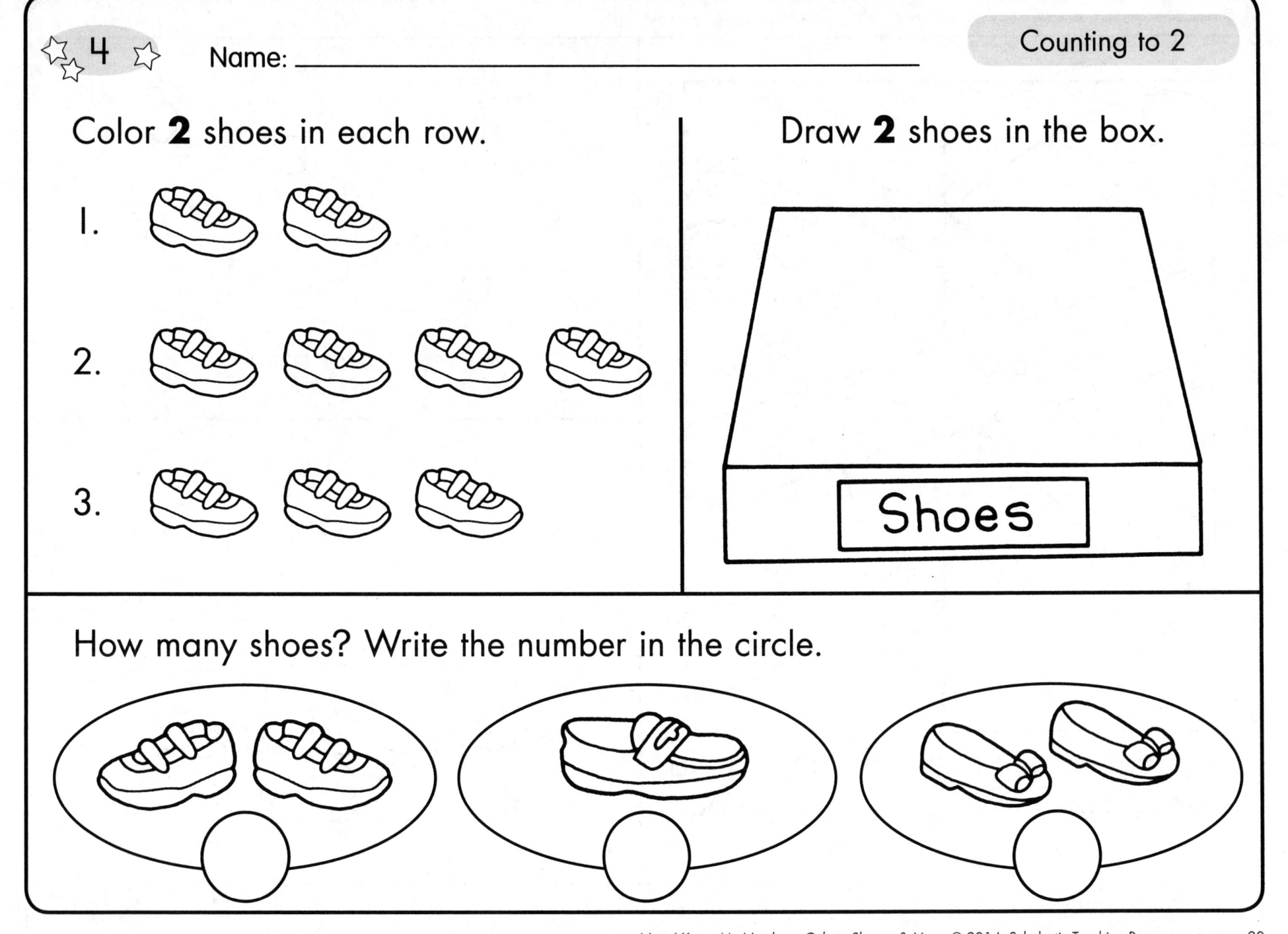

Name: _____

I one

Trace. Write.

one   one   one

one

Find each **one**. Color that sun.

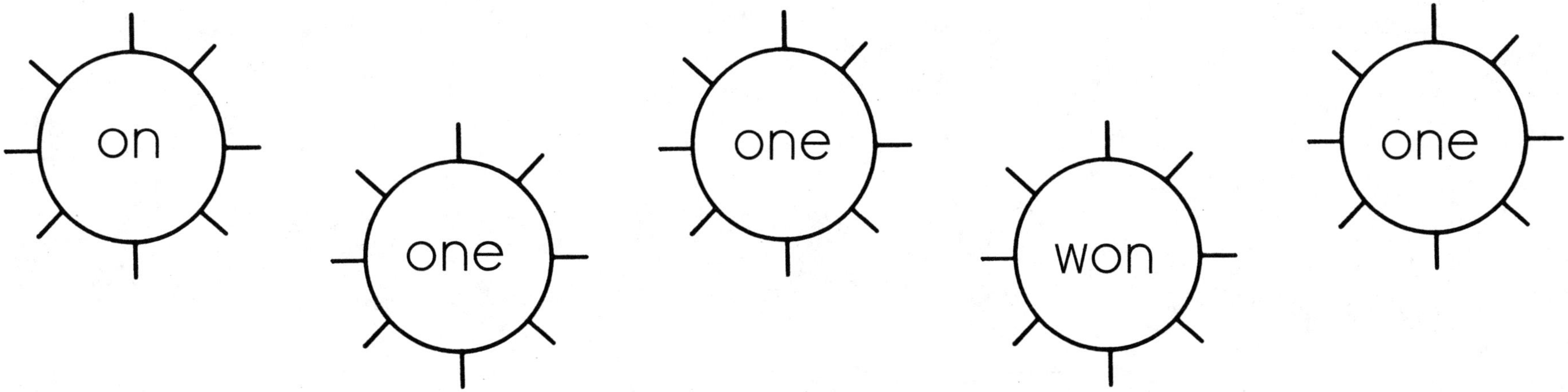

on

one

one

won

one

2 two

Trace. Write.

two   two   two

two

Find each **two**. Color that shoe.

two

two

tow

two

ton

Name: _____

3
three

Trace. Write.

3   3

Circle each **3**.

3   5   2
1   4
    6
3
2   3   3

Find each **3**. Color that space orange.
Then color the rest of the picture.

1   0
  3   3
4   1
  3   3
2   4
  3   3
3   3
0   2

Color **3** bees in each row.

Draw **3** bees on the flower.

1.

2.

3.

How many bees? Write the number in the box.

Name: _____

4
four

Trace. Write.

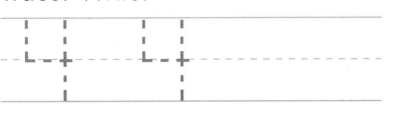

Find each 4. Color that space green. Then color the rest of the picture.

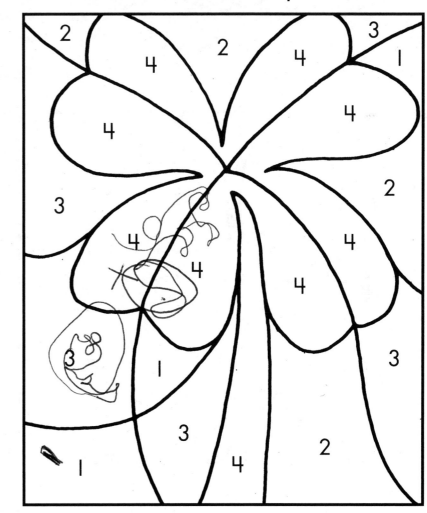

Circle each 4.

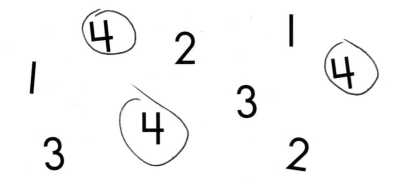

Color **4** clovers in each row.

1.

2.

3.

Draw **4** ladybugs on the clover.

How many ladybugs? Write the number on the line.

_____   _____   _____

Name: _____

3 three

Trace. Write.

three three three

three

Find each **three**. Color that bee.

tree

three

three

three

the

12 Name: _____

4 four

Trace. Write.

four four four

four

Find each **four**. Color that clover.

four

fan

four

four

for

5
five

Trace. Write.

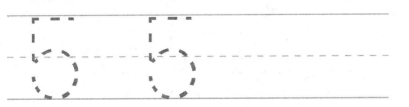

Circle each **5**. YOU

3

5   **2**   **3**

3

2   **5**   1

5   4

Find each **5**. Color that space yellow.
Then color the rest of the picture.

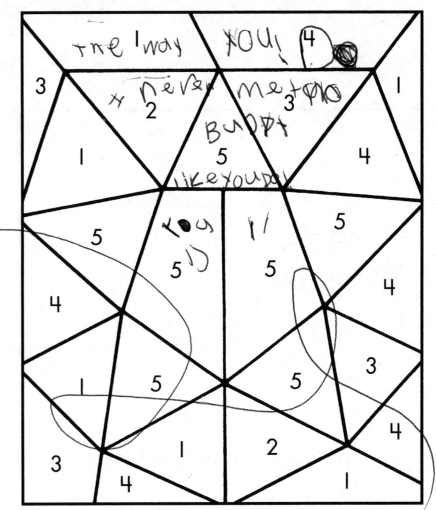

Name: _____

Color **5** stars in each row.

1. ☆ ☆ ☆ ☆ ☆ ☆ ☆

2. ☆ ☆ ☆ ☆ ☆

3. ☆ ☆ ☆ ☆ ☆ ☆

Draw **5** stars in the sky.

How many stars? Write the number in the circle.

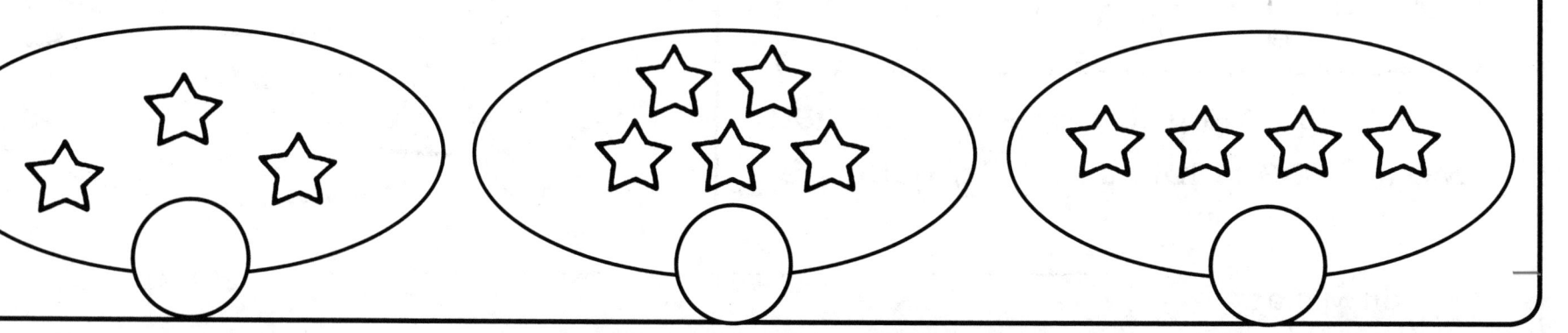

☆ 15 ☆ Name: _____

Trace. Write.

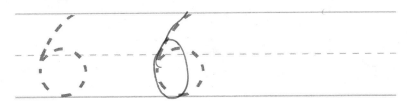

Circle each **6**.

4   6   1
6   5
      2
   3
0   6

Find each **6**. Color that space yellow.
Then color the rest of the picture.

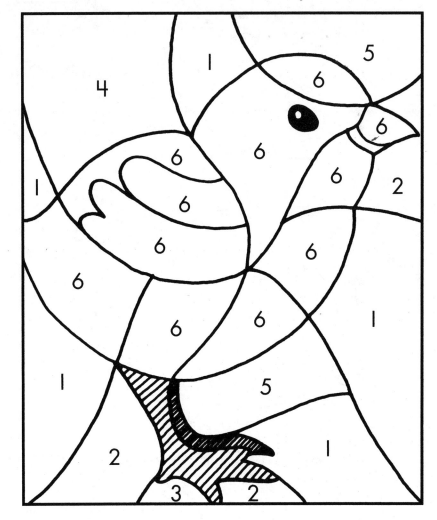

How many eggs? Write the number in the box.

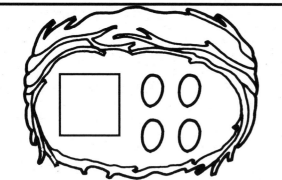
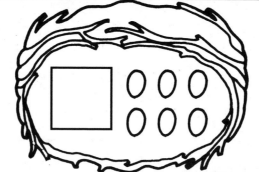
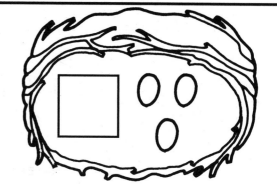

Draw **6** eggs in the nest.

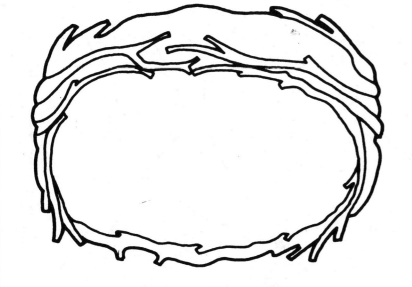

Color **6** chicks in each row.

1.

2.

3.

Name: _____

5 five

Trace. Write.

five
five
five

five

Find each **five**. Color that star.

fire

five

five

live

five

Name: _____

6 six

Trace. Write.

six   six   six   six

six

Find each **six**. Color that chick.

six   exit   six   six   sit

Name: _____

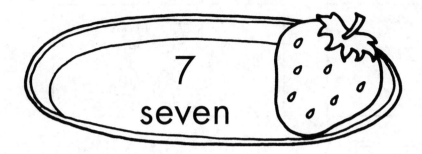

7
seven

Trace. Write.

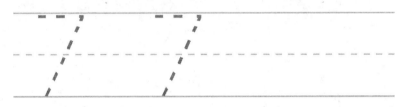

Circle each **7**.

5
6   2   3
         1   7
  7   7   4

Find each **7**. Color that space red.
Then color the rest of the picture.

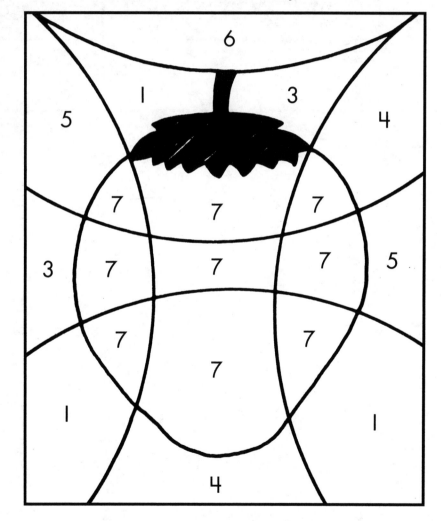

Color **7** strawberries.

Draw **7** seeds on the strawberry.

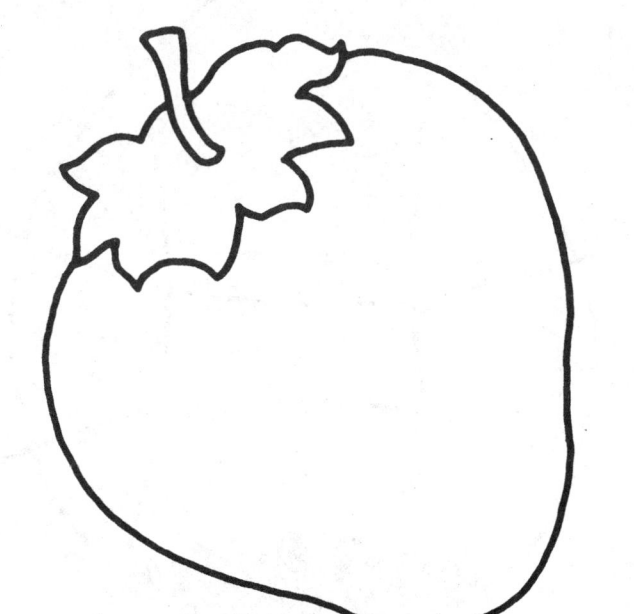

How many strawberries? Write the number in the box.

Name: _____

8
eight

Trace. Write.

8 8

Circle each 8.

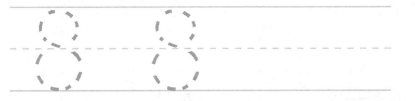

Find each **8**. Color that space pink.
Then color the rest of the picture.

☆ 22 ☆ Name: _____

Color 8 cupcakes.

Draw 8 candies on the cupcake.

How many candies? Write the number on the line.

_____   _____   _____

Name: _____

Trace. Write.

seven   seven

seven

Find each **seven**. Color that strawberry.

seven   seven   sent   even   seven

⭐ 24 ⭐ Name: _____

8 eight

Trace. Write.

eight   eight

eight

Find each **eight**. Color that cupcake.

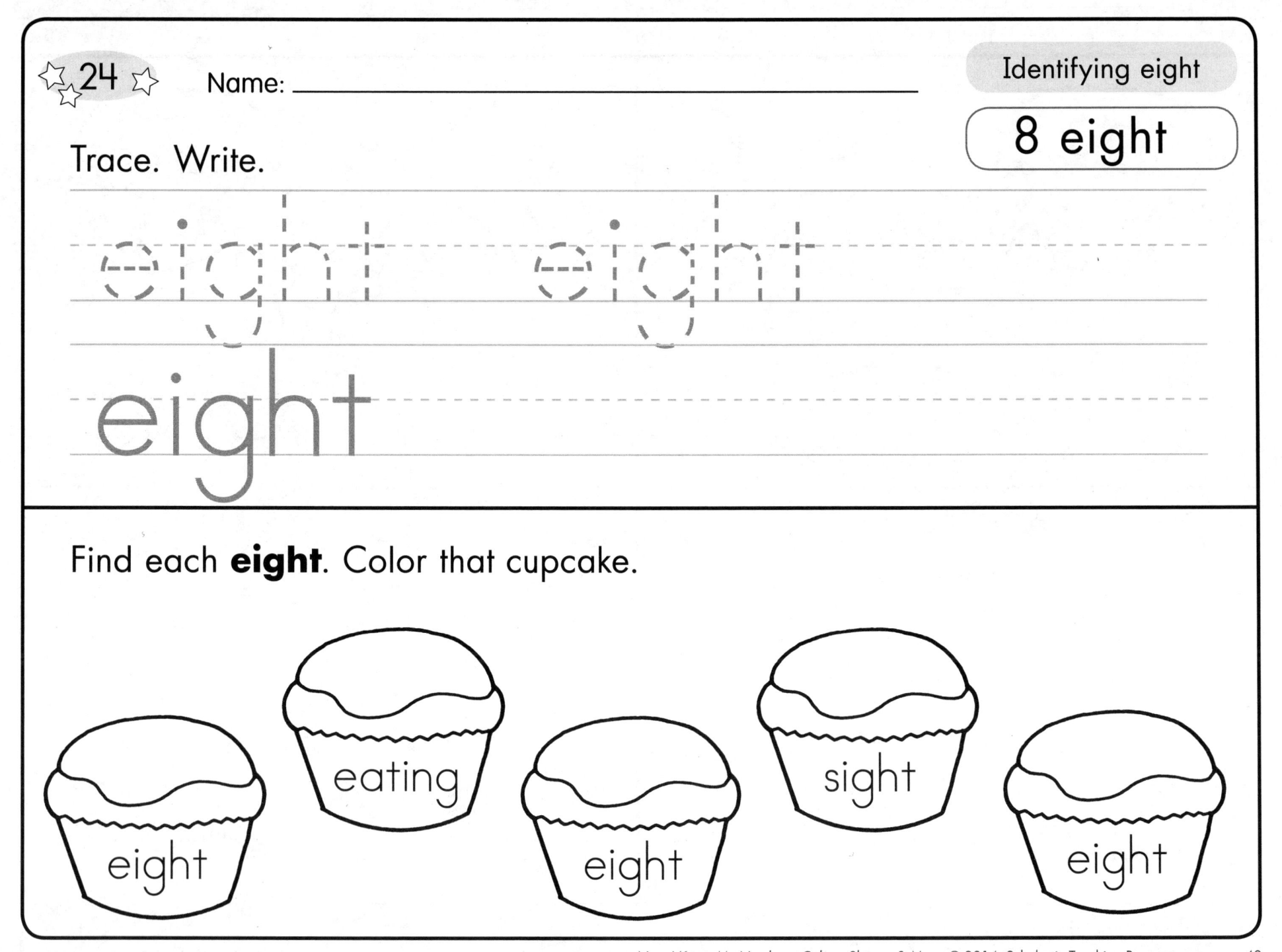

eight   eating   eight   sight   eight

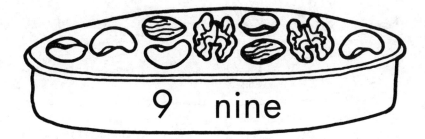

9   nine

Trace. Write.

Circle each **9**.

6   4   9

0   6

7   9

9   3

Find each **9**. Color that space brown. Then color the rest of the picture.

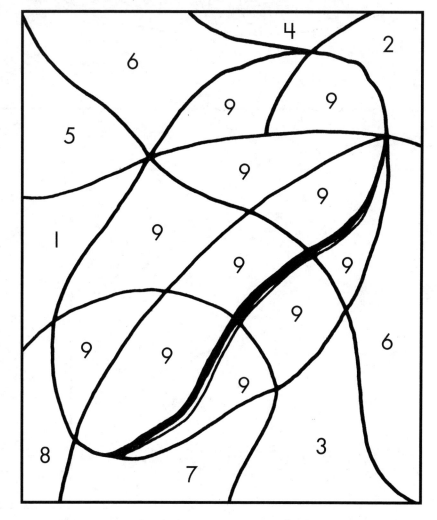

Name: _____

Color **9** nuts.

Draw **9** nuts in the hand.

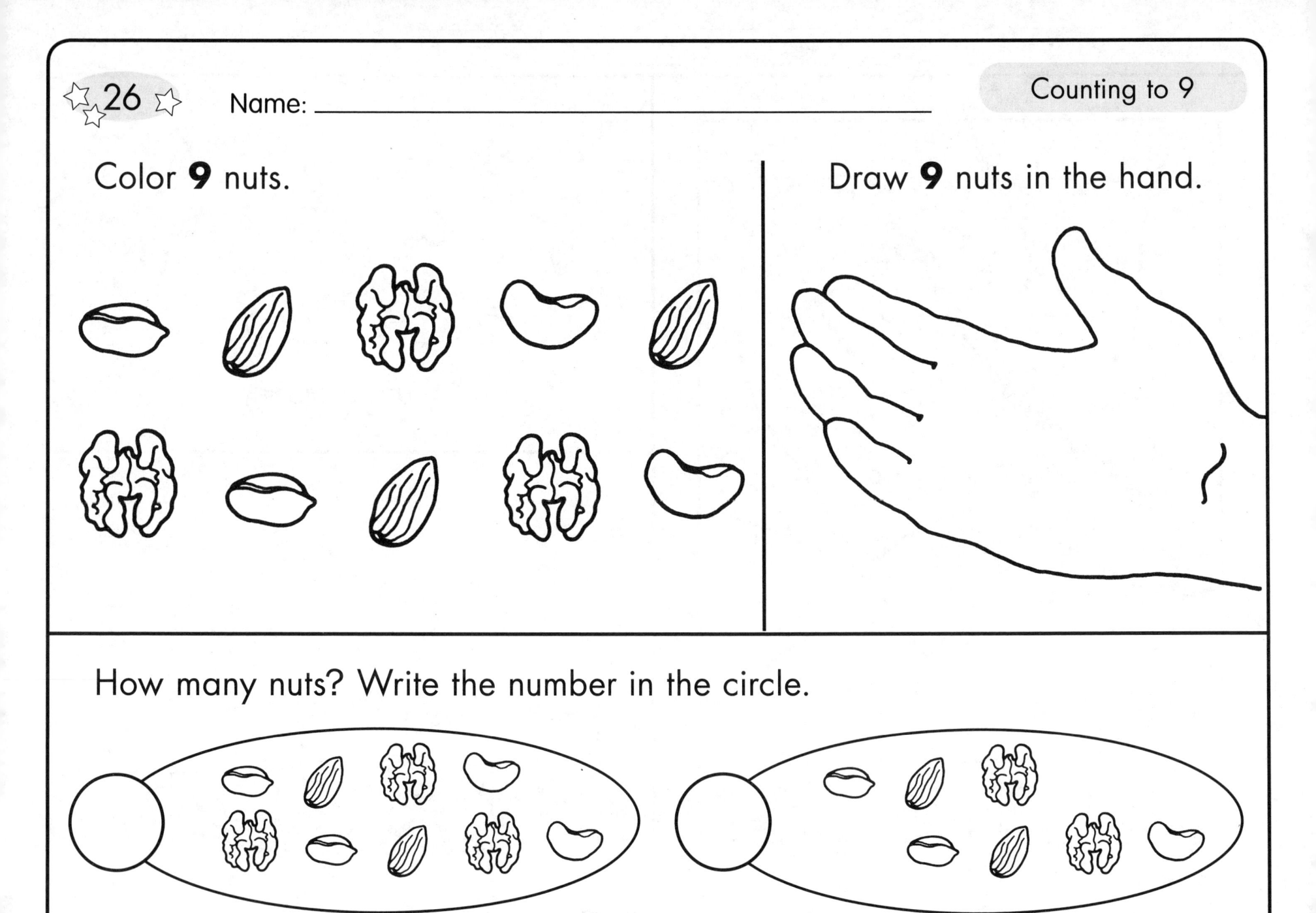

How many nuts? Write the number in the circle.

Name: _____

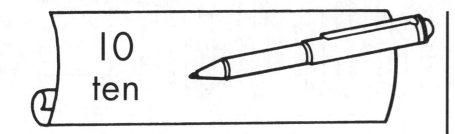

10
ten

Find each **10**. Color that space blue. Then color the rest of the picture.

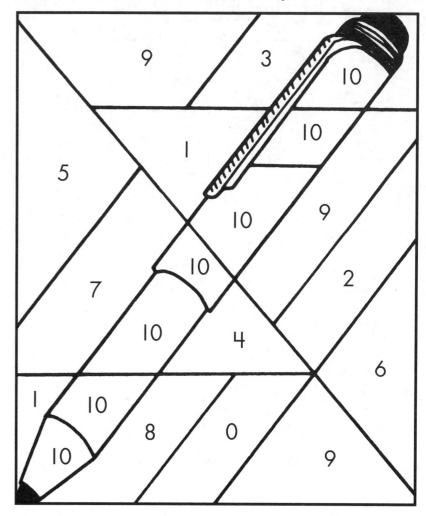

Trace. Write.

Circle each **10**.

10   6   10   0

10   3

        1

2   8   10

Color **10** pens.

Draw **10** pens in the box.

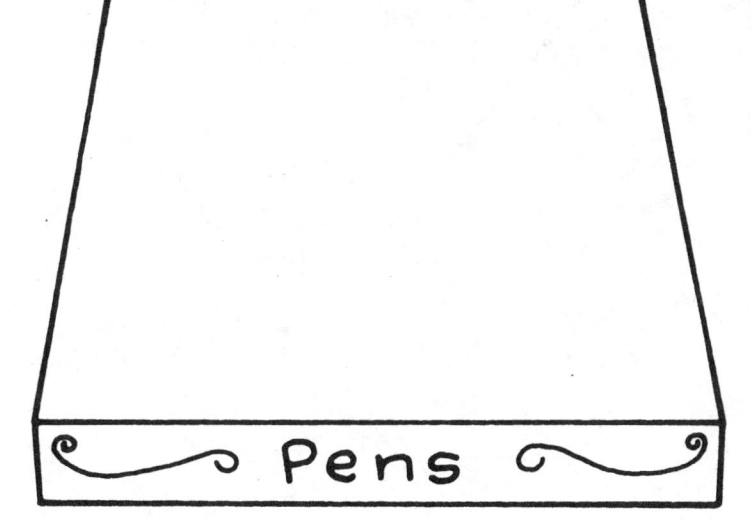

How many pens? Write the number in the box.

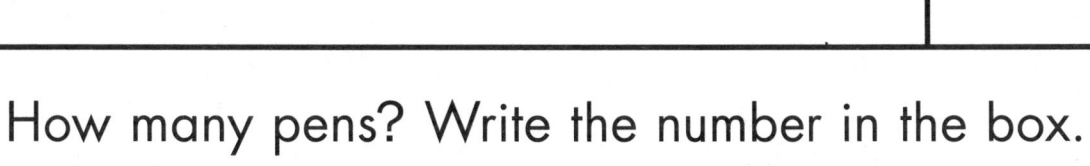

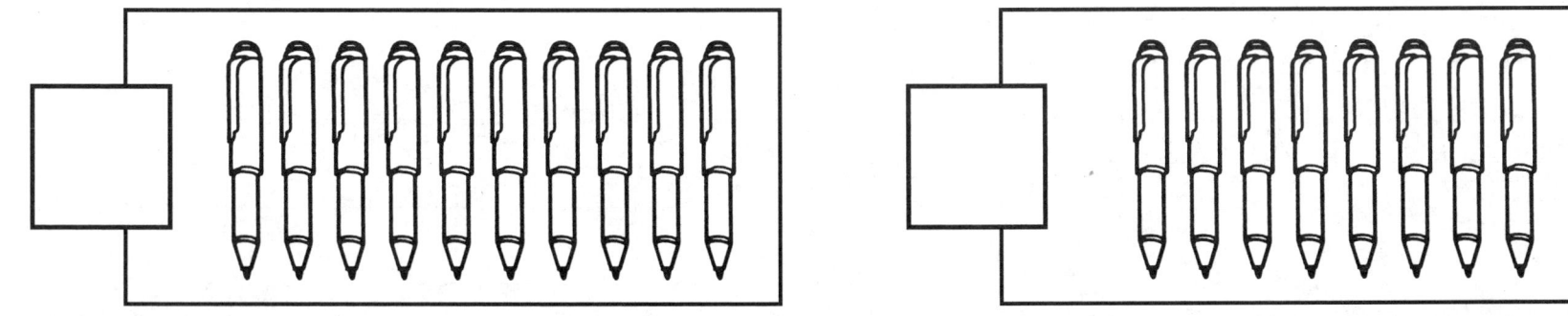

Name: _____

9 nine

Trace. Write.

nine   nine   nine

nine

Find each **nine**. Color that nut.

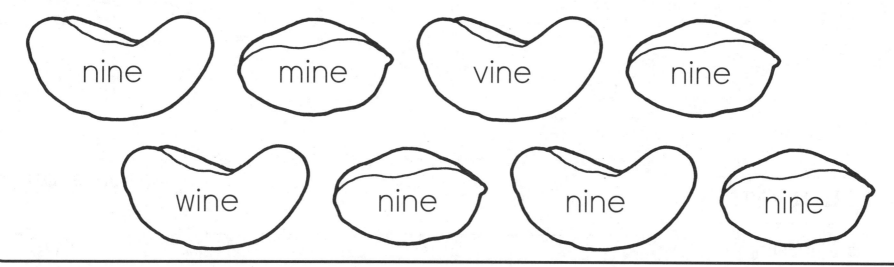

nine   mine   vine   nine

wine   nine   nine   nine

Name: _____

10 ten

Trace. Write.

ten   ten   ten

ten

Find each **ten**. Color that pen.

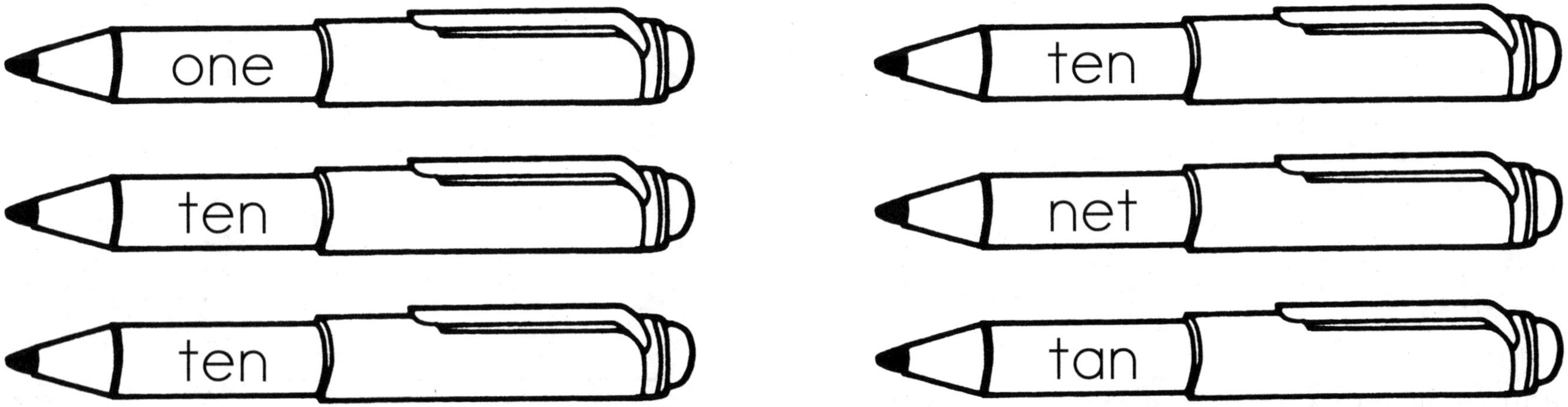

one	ten
ten	net
ten	tan

Name: _____

11
eleven

Trace. Write.

| | | |

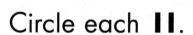
eleven

Circle each **11**.

9 11 7 11 2
5 11 10 4

Find each **11**. Color that space red. Then color the rest of the picture.

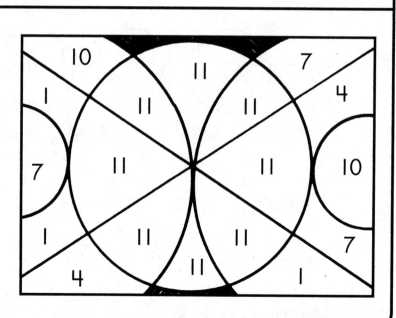

☆32☆ Name: _____

Color 11 balls.

How many balls? Write the number in the box.

Name: _____

12
twelve

Trace. Write.

12 12

twelve

Circle each **12**.

4   12   1

12   11

2   10   7   12

Find each **12**. Color that space pink. Then color the rest of the picture.

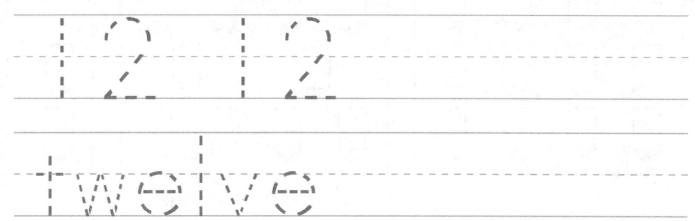

Name: _____

Color **12** gifts.

How many gifts? Write the number in the box.

Name: _____

13
thirteen

Trace. Write.

13 13

thirteen

Circle each **13**.

3

13

8

13

13

10

11

13

12

1

Find each **13**. Color that space red. Then color the rest of the picture.

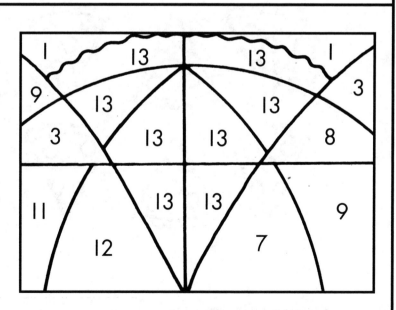

 36

Name: _____

Color 13 pizza slices.

How many pizza slices? Write the number in the box.

14
fourteen

Trace. Write.

Circle each **14**.

10   14   4

11   12

        1

14   13   14

Find each **14**. Color that space yellow. Then color the rest of the picture.

1	13	14	14	10	4
12		14		14	11
9					8
4		14	14		13
10	14			14	4

How many candles? Write the number in the box.

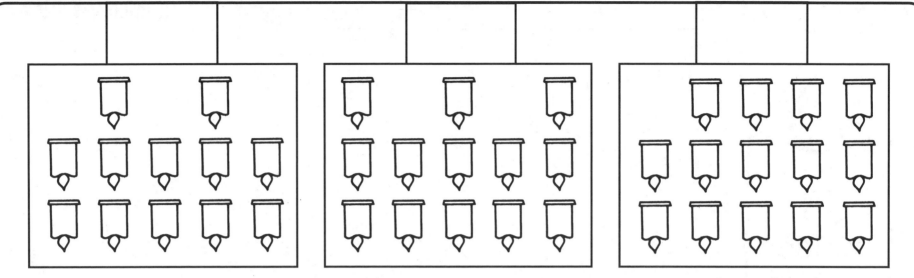

Color **14** candles.

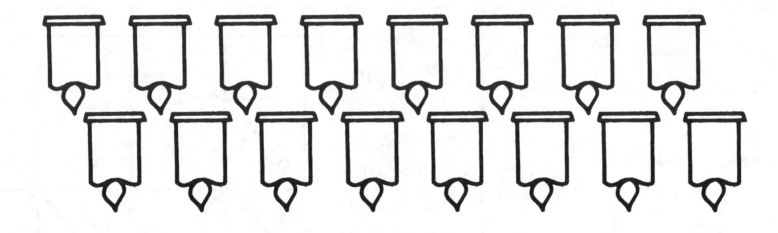

Name: _____

☆ **38** ☆

Counting to 14

☆ 39 ☆ Name: _____

15
fifteen

Trace. Write.

15 15

fifteen

Circle each **15**.

15   1
5   12
15
11   15   10
15
14

Find each **15**. Color that space purple. Then color the rest of the picture.

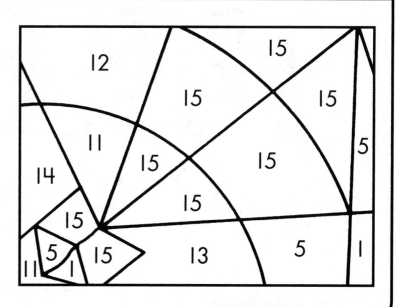

Name: _____

☆ 40 ☆☆

Color **15** kites.

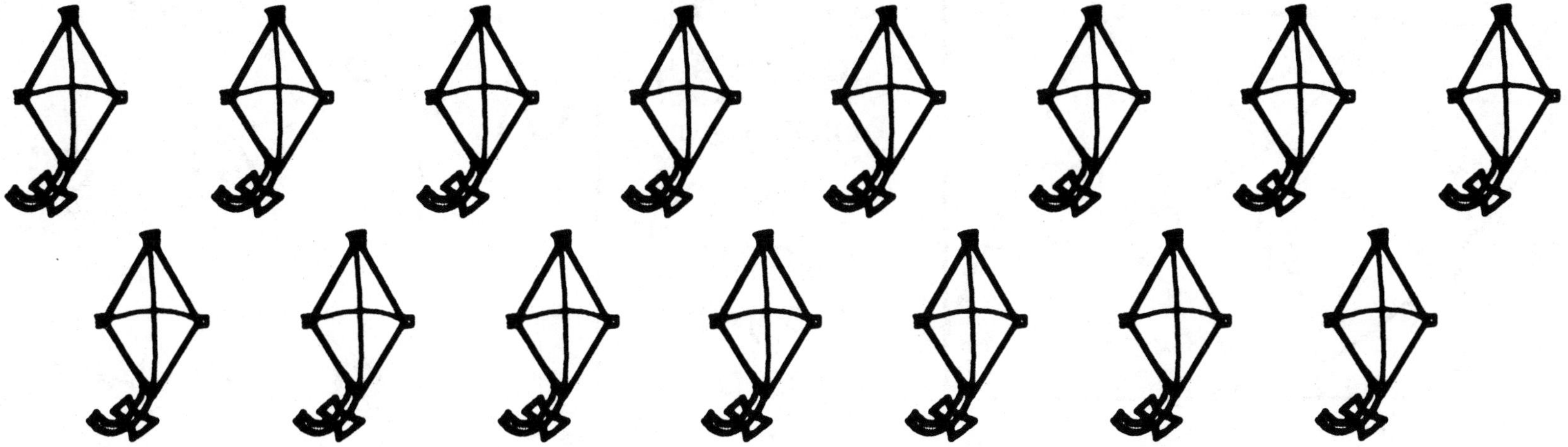

How many kites? Write the number in the box.

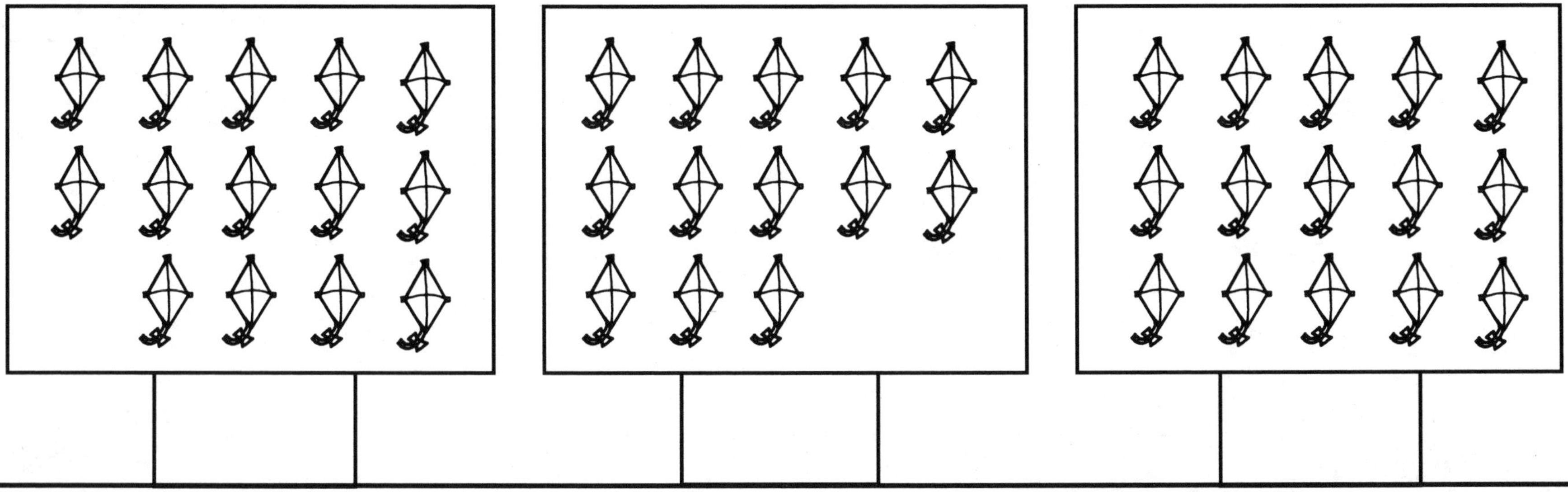

Name: _____

Trace. Write.

16 16

sixteen

16
sixteen

Circle each **16**.

10   1   9   16   12

16   8   16   6

Find each **16**. Color that space red. Then color the rest of the picture.

10		11
13	16	16	6
10	16	16	9
9	16	16	13
11	16	16	10
1		8	

Name: _____

Color 16 hearts.

Counting to 16

How many hearts? Write the number in the box.

Name: _____

17

seventeen

Trace. Write.

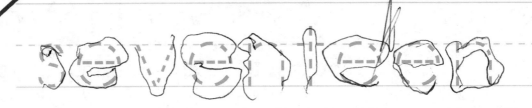

Circle each **17**.

Find each **17**. Color that space yellow. Then color the rest of the picture.

	14		7
12		17	
			11
	17		
11			17
	17		13
		17	
7	17		15
	1		

Name: _____

44

Color **17** stars.

How many stars? Write the number in the box.

☆45☆ Name: _____

18
eighteen

Trace. Write.

18   18

eighteen

Circle each **18**.

1
18   16
15   8
12
18   10
18   18

Find each **18**. Color that space green. Then color the rest of the picture.

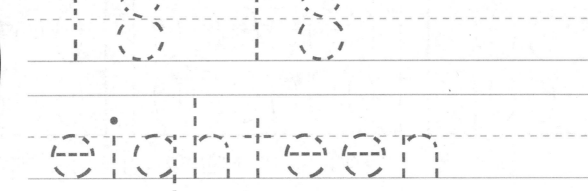

Counting to 18

☆ 46 ☆

Color **18** ovals.

How many ovals? Write the number in the box.

Name: _____

Trace. Write.

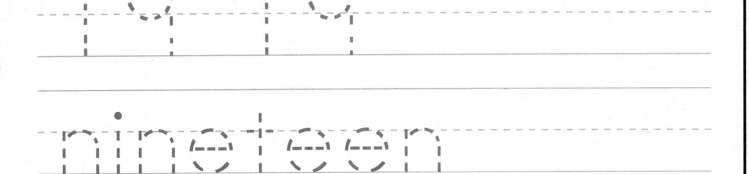

19
nineteen

Circle each **19**.

19   1   17
18   9
16
10
19   19

Find each **19**. Color that space red. Then color the rest of the picture.

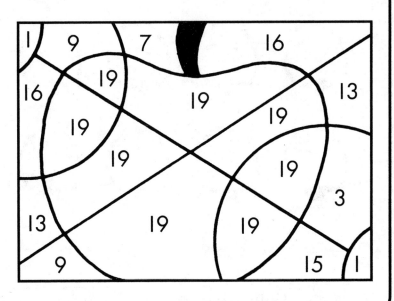

Name: _____

Color **19** apples.

How many apples? Write the number in the box.

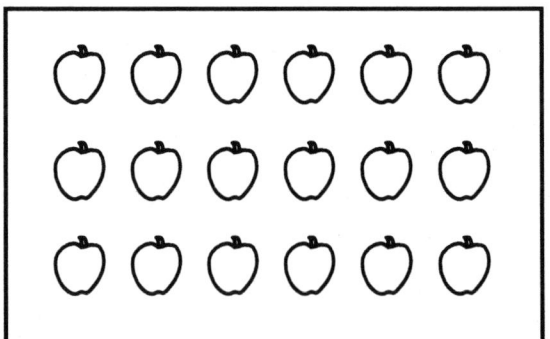

Name: _____

20
twenty

Trace. Write.

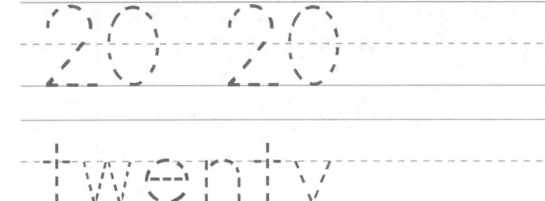

20   20

twenty

Circle each **20**.

12   2   20   10   19

20   17   0   20

Find each **20**. Color that space green. Then color the rest of the picture.

	10		20
1		20	20
12	20		20
	20		20
19		20	20	19
20	1		2	0

How many leaves? Write the number in the box.

☆50☆

Color **20** leaves.

Name: _____

21
twenty-one

Trace. Write.

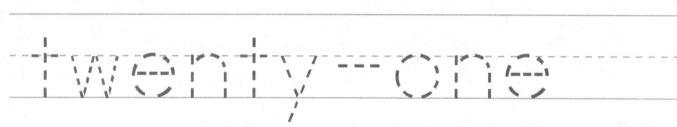

Circle each **21**.

21   10   19

12   11

22   21   20

21

Find each **21**. Color that space orange. Then color the rest of the picture.

12		11
11	21	20
	21	
20	21	12
11	21	10

21 21 21 21 21 21 21 21

How many flowers? **Write the number in the box.**

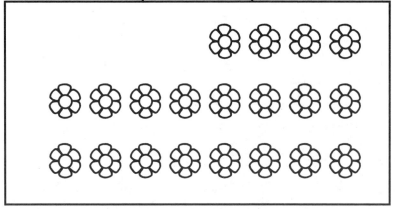

Color **21** flowers.

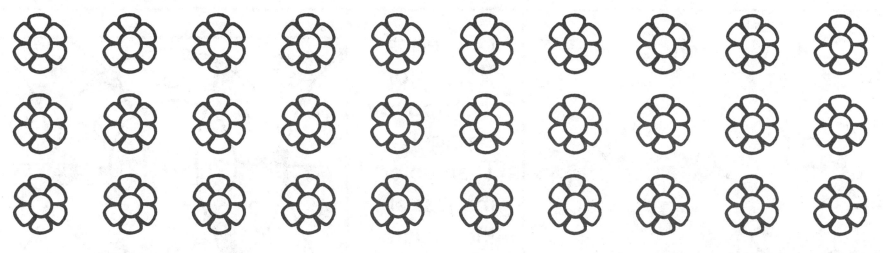

Name: _____

21

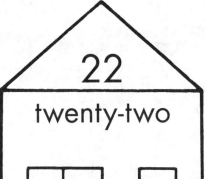

22
twenty-two

Trace. Write.

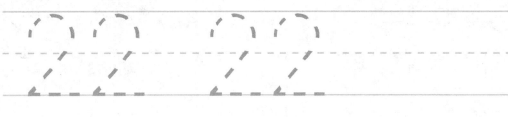

Circle each **22**.

10   22   21

22   2

     15

20   12   22

Find each **22**. Color that space brown. Then color the rest of the picture.

21	18	22	22	15	2
12	22		22		17
19		22			
		22	22	22	20

 **54**

Name: _____

Color **22** houses.

How many houses? Write the number in the box.

☆ 55 ☆ Name: _____

23
twenty-three

Trace. Write.

23 23

twenty-three

Circle each **23**.

23   8   13   23
         23   2
   3 23
20   18

Find each **23**. Color that space brown. Then color the rest of the picture.

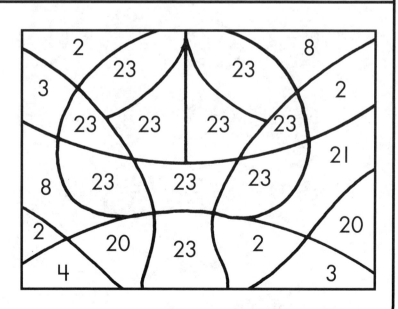

☆56☆

Name: _____

Color **23** mushrooms.

How many mushrooms? **Write the number in the box.**

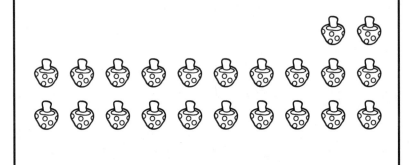

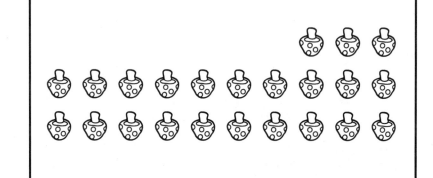

Name: _____

Trace. Write.

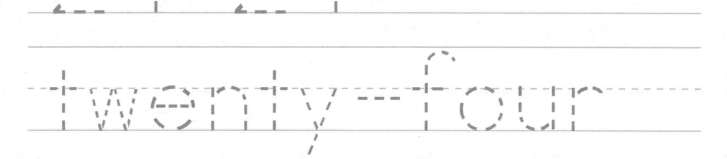

24
twenty-four

Circle each **24**.

22   24   13
21   12
        20
24   14   24

Find each **24**. Color that space purple. Then color the rest of the picture.

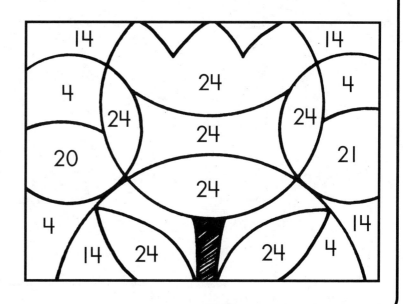

How many flowers? Write the number in the box.

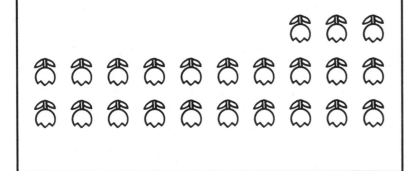

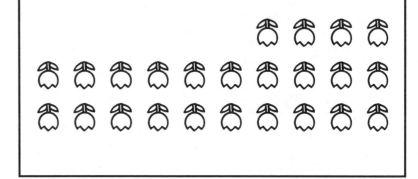

Color **24** flowers.

Name: _____

Name: _____

25
twenty-five

Trace. Write.

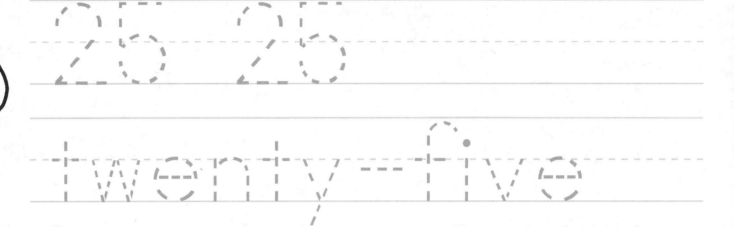

Circle each **25**.

25   20   15
23   22
        25
    25   24
5

Find each **25**. Color that space green. Then color the rest of the picture.

Counting to 25

How many trees? Write the number in the box.

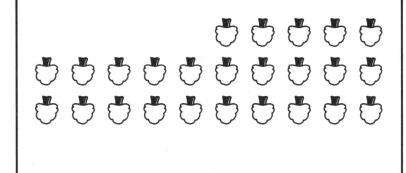

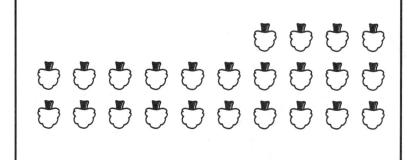

Color **25** trees.

Name: _____

Name: _____

26
twenty-six

Trace. Write.

26 26

twenty-six

Circle each **26**.

12 26 26

2 20

23

26 19 16

Find each **26**. Color that space blue. Then color the rest of the picture.

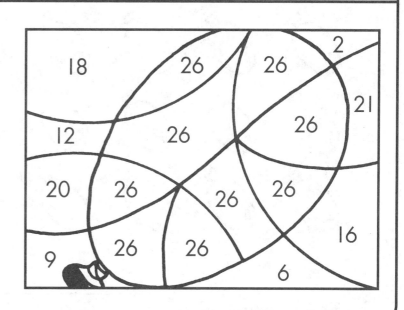

Counting to 26

Name:

How many balloons? Write the number in the box.

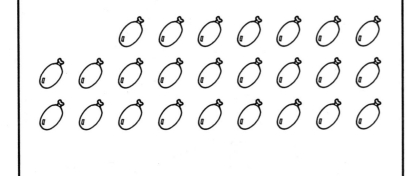

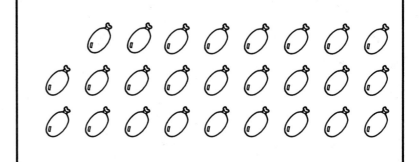

Color **26** balloons.

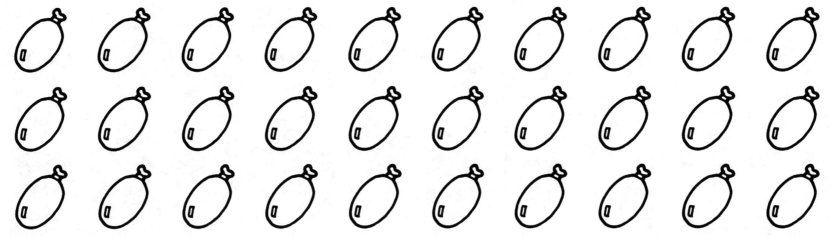

Name:

Name: _____

27

twenty-seven

Trace. Write.

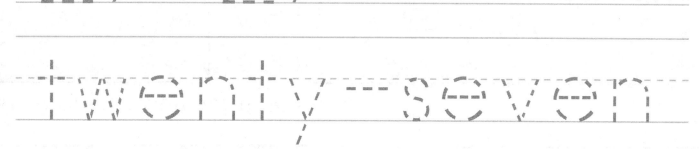

Circle each **27**.

27   7   20

26   22

12   27   17   27

Find each **27**. Color that space red. Then color the rest of the picture.

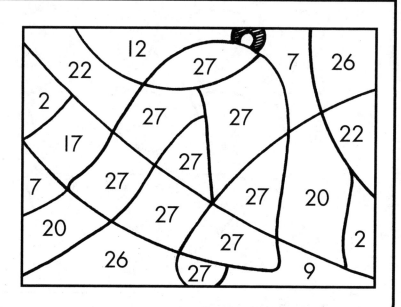

64 Name: _____

Color **27** bells.

How many bells? Write the number in the box.

28
twenty-eight

Trace. Write.

28 28

twenty-eight

Circle each **28**.

28   8   28
23   13
20   28   18   26

Find each **28**. Color that space purple. Then color the rest of the picture.

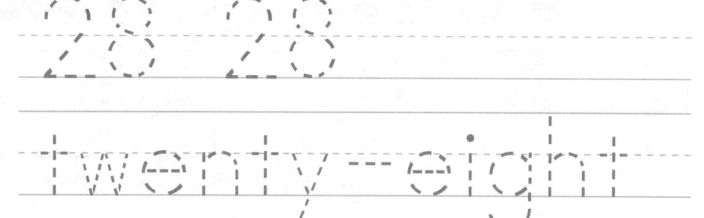

 **66**

Name: _____

Color **28** eggs.

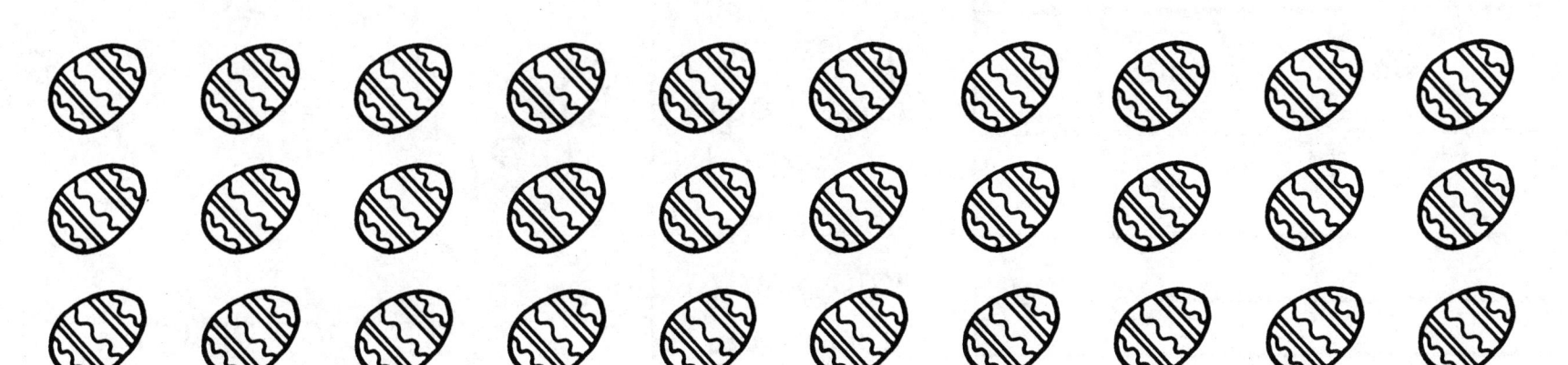

How many eggs? Write the number in the box.

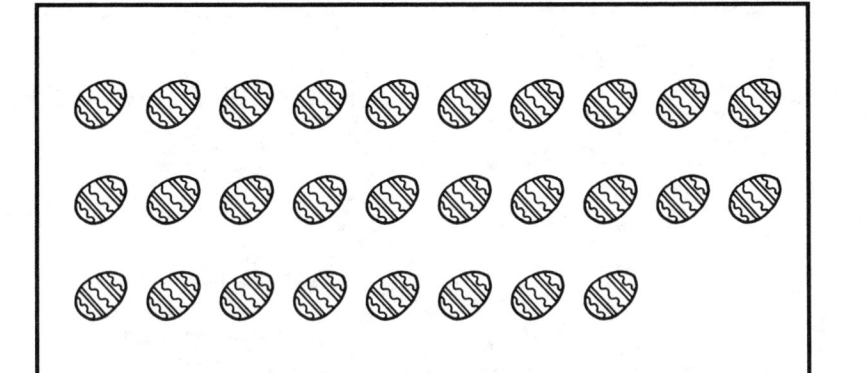

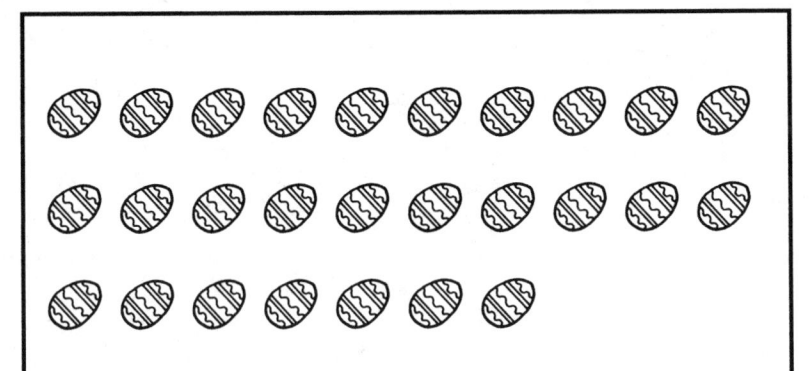

29
twenty-nine

Trace. Write.

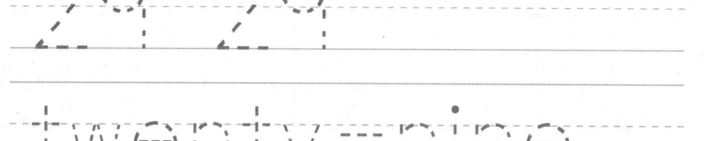

Circle each **29**.

29   20   16
18   29
        9
29   26   19

Find each **29**. Color that space pink. Then color the rest of the picture.

2	6			2	9
26	29	29	29		19
19		29	29		20
	29		29		
		29		29	
9	29		29	6	28
	2				

Counting to 29

How many shells? Write the number in the box.

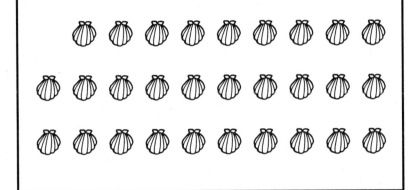

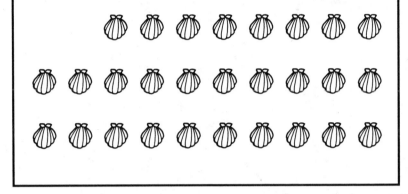

Name: _____

Color **29** shells.

Name: _____

Trace. Write.

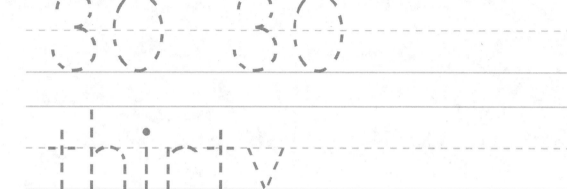

Circle each **30**.

30   20   10
13   3
       2
   23
30   30

Find each **30**. Color that space blue. Then color the rest of the picture.

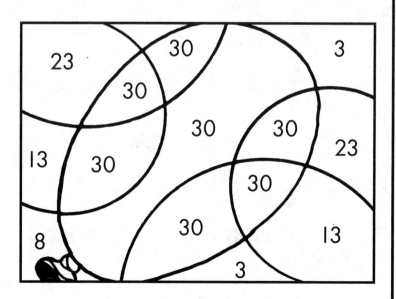

Color **30** balloons.

Connect the dots. Start at 19.

30 ● —— ● 19

29 ●   ● 20

28 ●   ● 21

27 ●   ● 22

26 ●   ● 23

25 ●● 24

Name: _____

40
forty

Trace. Write.

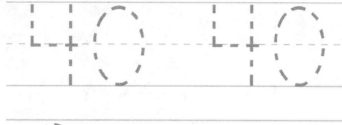

Circle each **40**.

40

14   34

24   10

4

30

40   40

Find each **40**. Color that space pink. Then color the rest of the picture.

2	30	40	40	10	21
14	40			24
3	40	40	40	2
24	40		40	14
8	34	40	8	2
	1	4	

☆ **72** ☆

Name: _____

Counting to 40

Color **40** acorns.

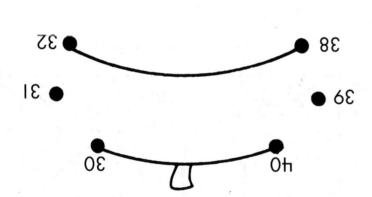

Connect the dots. Start at 30.

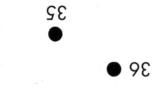

30 31 32 33 34 35 36 37 38 39 40

Trace. Write.

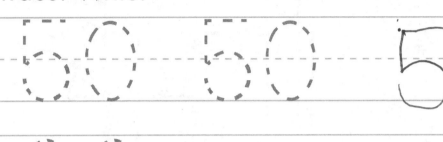

50 50 50

fifty

50
fifty

Circle each **50**.

20
35   50   45
15   50   5   25
     50   50

Find each **50**. Color that space blue. Then color the rest of the picture.

1	50		20	30	
5	50	50	50	50	4
1	50	50	50	50	1
	15	2			5

Name: _____

Color **50** flags.

Connect the dots. Start at 40.

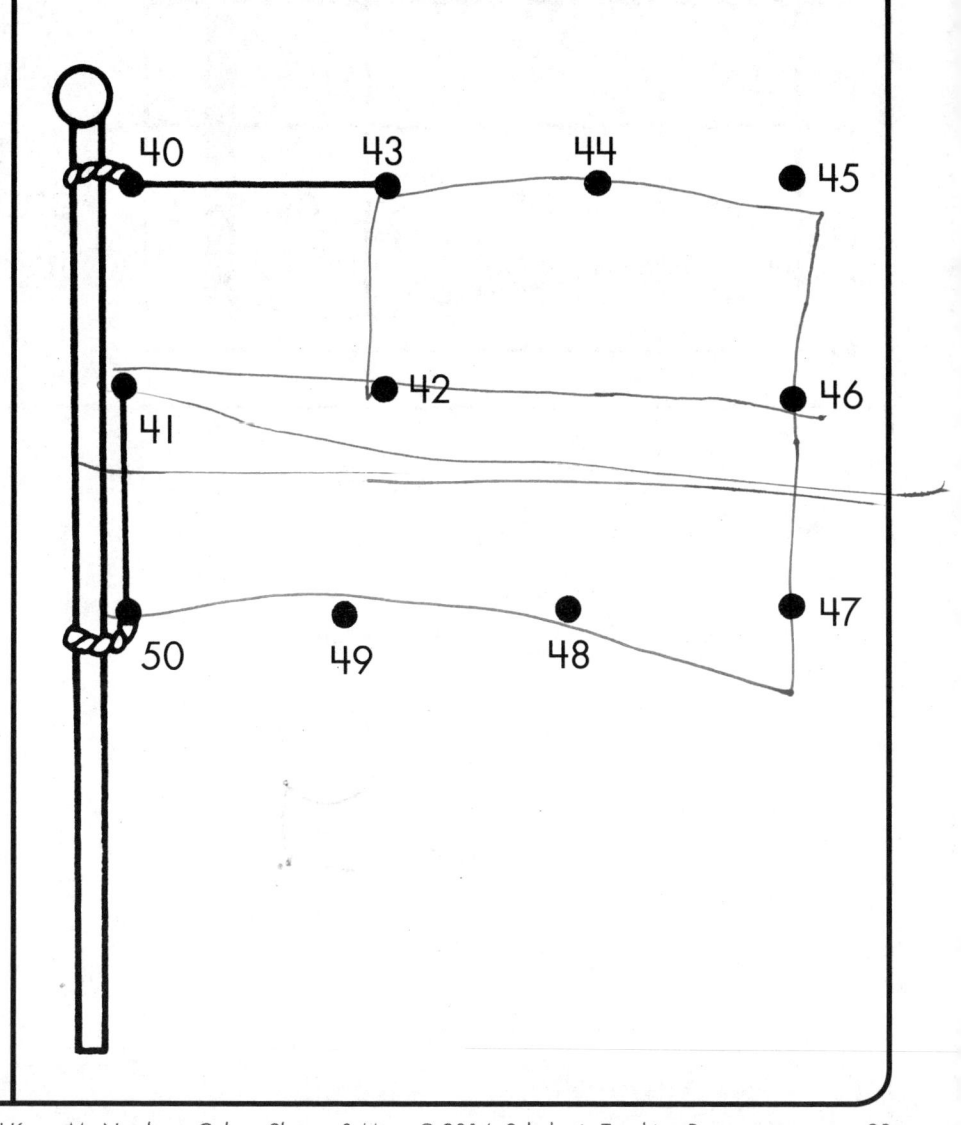

☆ 75 ☆ Name: _____

60
sixty

Trace. Write.

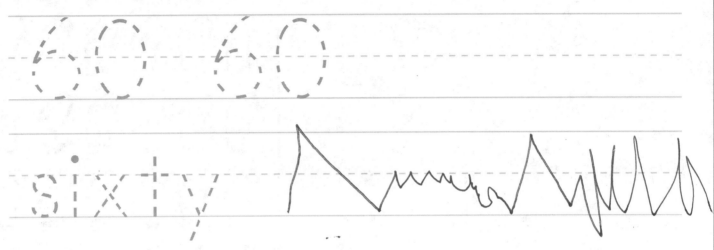

60   60

sixty

Circle each **60**.

56
46   36
60   60
       6
16   20
          60

Find each **60**. Color that space brown. Then color the rest of the picture.

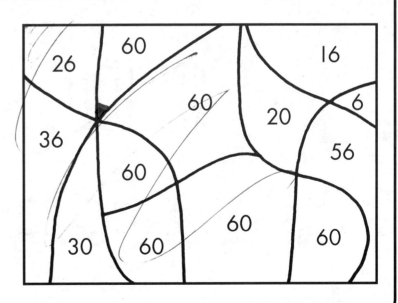

26   60   16
36   60   6
              20
      60   56
30 60   60   60

Connect the dots. Start at 50.

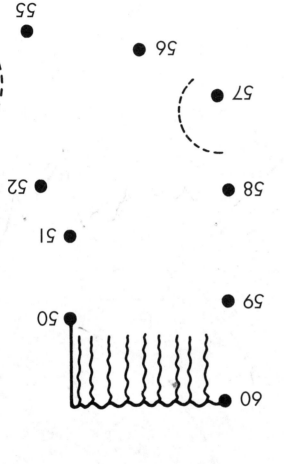

55
56
54
57
53
52
58
51
50
59
60

Color **60** socks.

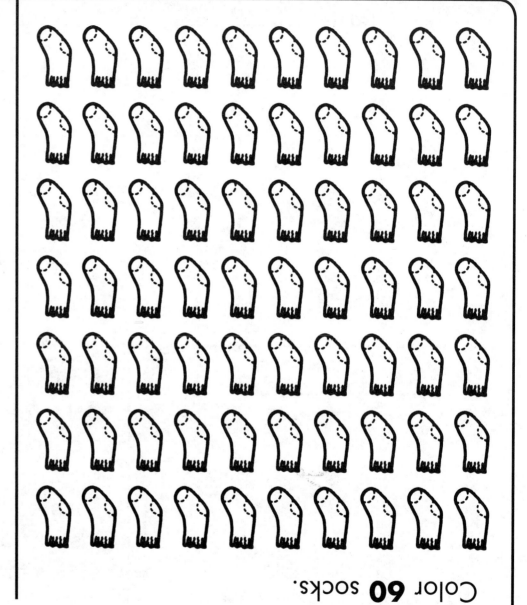

76

Name: _____

Trace. Write.

70
seventy

70 70

seventy

Circle each **70**.

7

57

70

17

47

20

40

70

70

70

Find each **70**. Color that space red. Then color the rest of the picture.

Counting to 70

Connect the dots. Start at 60.

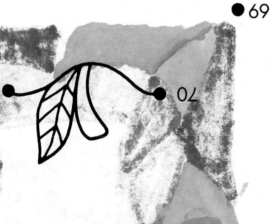

61 • 62 • 63 • 64 • 65 • 66 • 67 • 68 • 69 • 60 • 70

Name: _____

☆ 78 ☆

Color **70** apples.

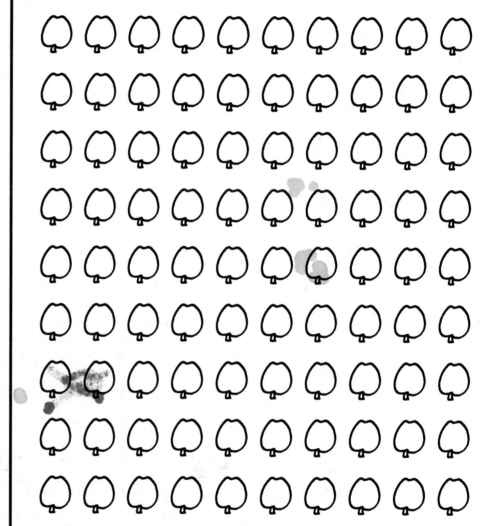

80
eighty

Trace. Write.

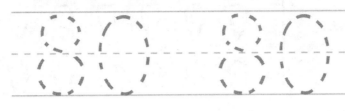

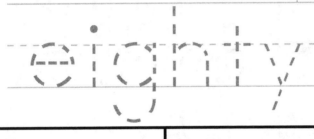

Circle each **80**.

Find each **80**. Color that space orange. Then color the rest of the picture.

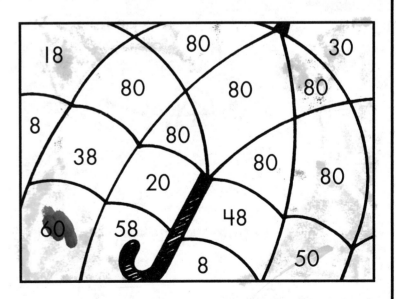

Color **80** raindrops.

Connect the dots. Start at 70.

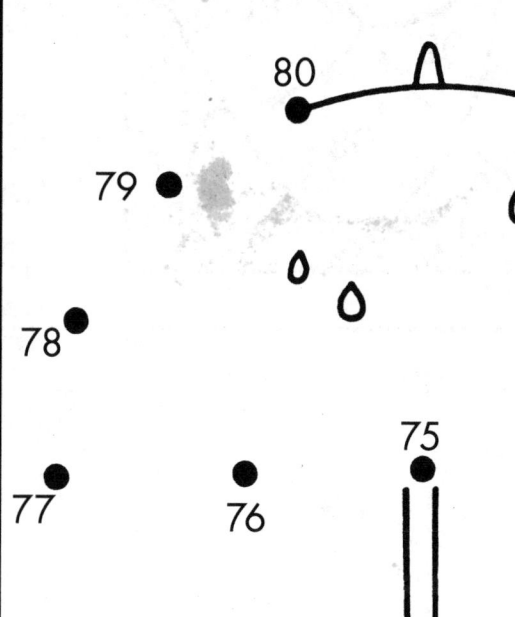

Trace. Write.

90 90

ninety

90
ninety

Circle each **90**.

9
70   19   90
    60   89
39   90   90

Find each **90**. Color that space green. Then color the rest of the picture.

9	50	30
90		80
40	90	89
90	90	
70	90	19
	90	90
20	90	30
	9	

☆ 82 ☆ Name: _____

Color **90** leaves.

Connect the dots. Start at 80.

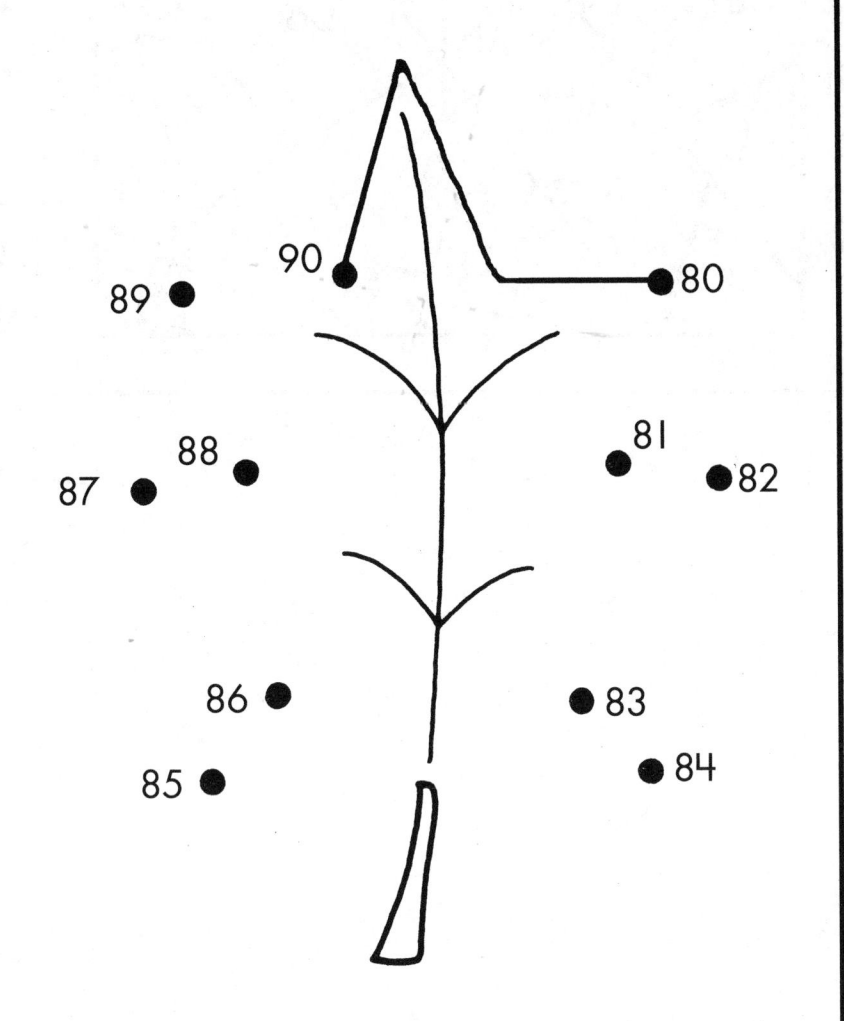

89 90 80

88 81
87 82

86 83

85 84

☆ 83 ☆

Name: _____

100

one hundred

Trace.

100   100

one hundred

Circle each **100**.

100
    10   80
11   17
        I
100   70   100

Find each **100**. Color that space yellow. Then color the rest of the picture.

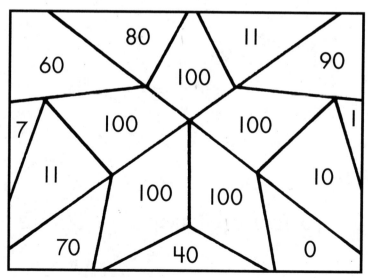

80   11
60   100   90
7   100   100   1
11   10
    100   100
70   40   0

Name: ____________________

Color **100** stars.

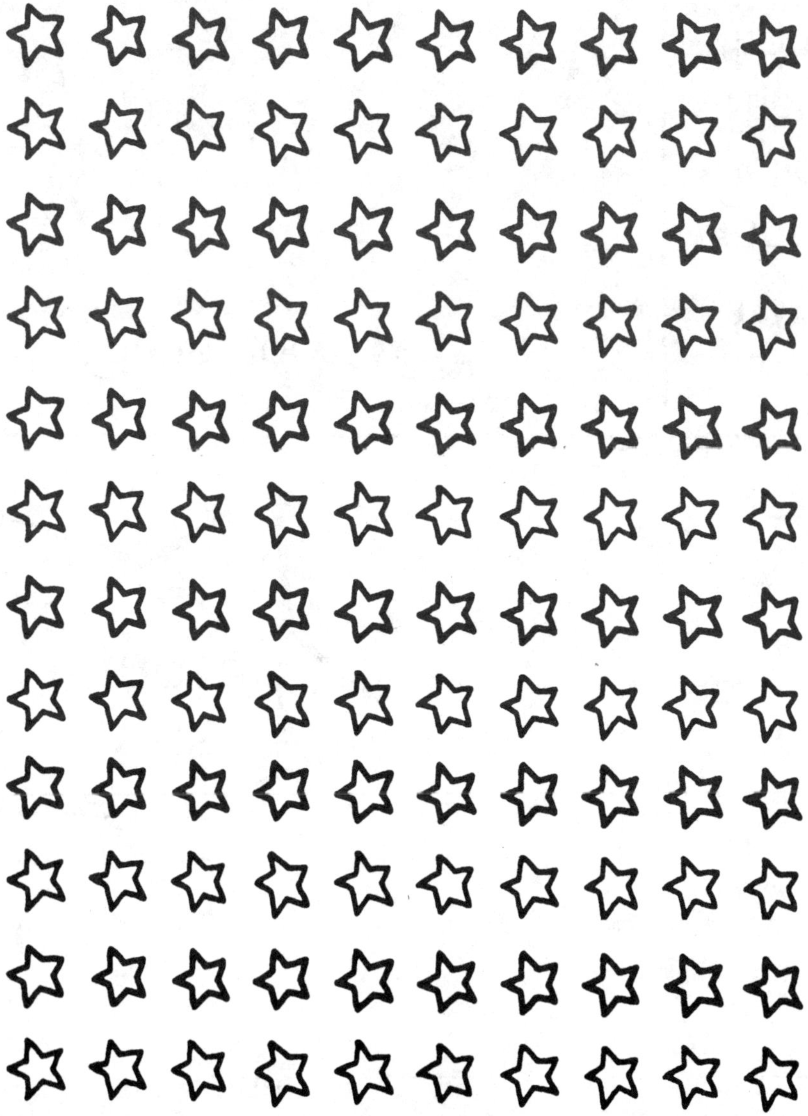

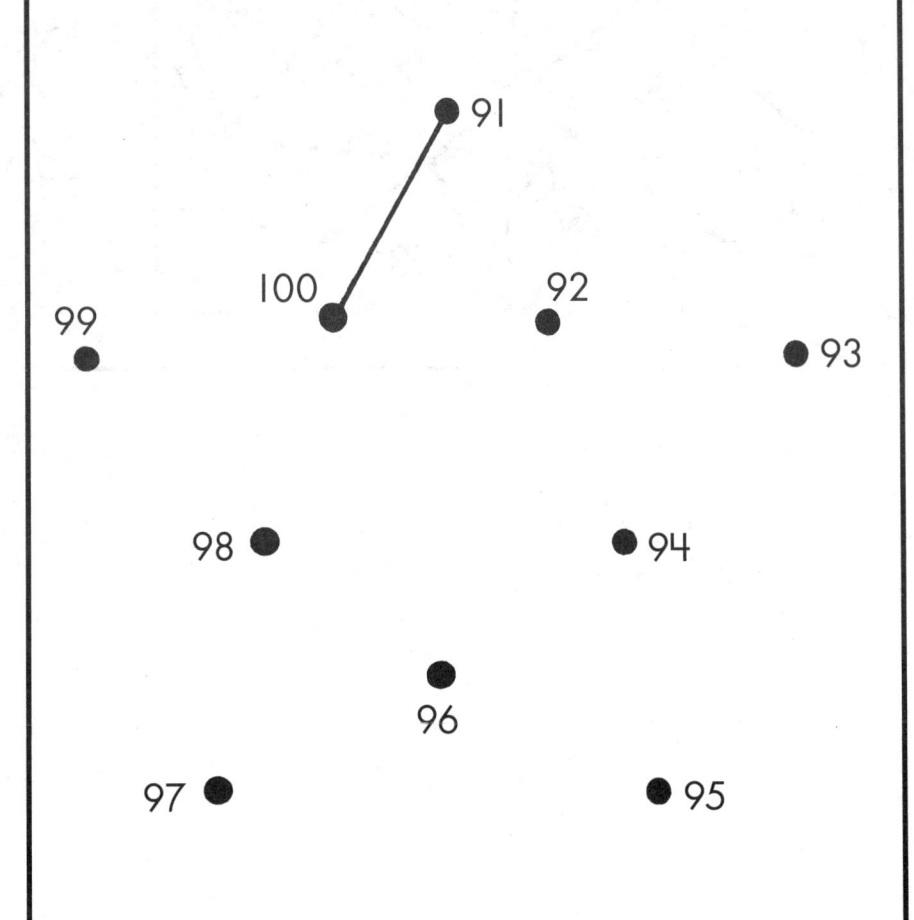

Connect the dots. Start at 91.

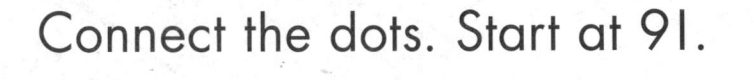

Name: _____

Write the missing numbers in each row. Color the **even** numbers.

Row 1: 1 __ 3 4 __ 6

Row 2: 10 __ __ 13 __ 15

Row 3: 18 __ 20 __ 22 __

Name: _____

Write the missing numbers in each row. Color the **even** numbers.

30   32   33   35

51   54   56

82   84   86

Name: _____

Odd Numbers

Write the missing numbers in each row. Color the **odd** numbers.

  3   5  6   8

  12    15   17

  25   27   29

Now I Know My Numbers, Colors, Shapes & More © 2014 Scholastic Teaching Resources • page 103

Name: _____

Write the missing numbers in each row. Color the **odd** numbers.

40   ( )   42   43   ( )   45

72   ( )   ( )   75   ( )   77

93   ( )   95   ( )   97   ( )

Count the flowers in each set. Write the number in the box.

Name: _____

Count the eggs in each set. Write the number in the box.

Count the raindrops in each set. Write the number in the box.

Counting Practice to 30

Name: _____

☆92☆

Count the fish in each set. Write the number in the box.

Count the stars in each set. Write the number in the box.

94

Name: _____

Count the apples in each set. Write the number in the box.

Name: _____

Compare the sets in each pair. Color the set that has **more**.

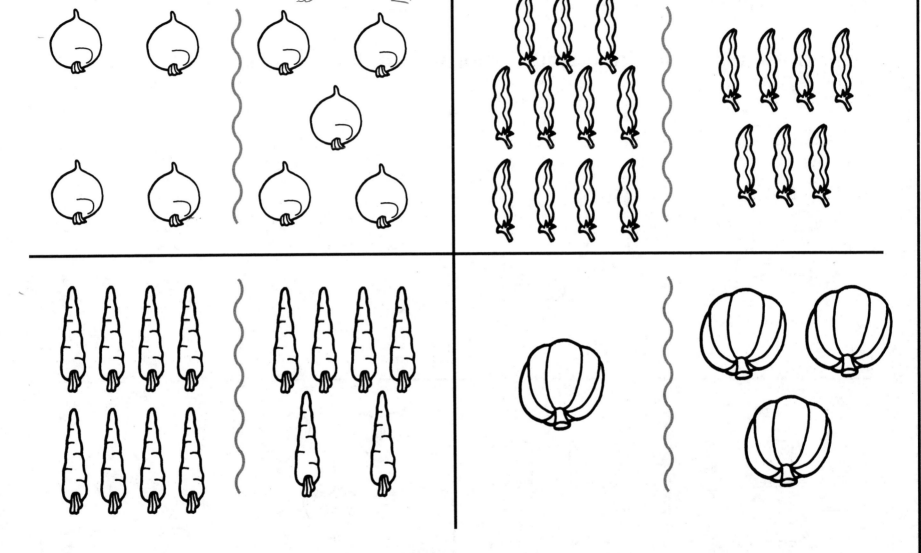

Compare the sets in each pair. Color the set that has more.

Name: _____

Comparing Sets: More

Name: _Zoev okm_

Compare the sets in each pair. Color the set that has **fewer**.

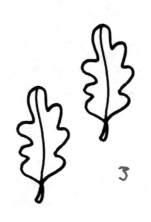 3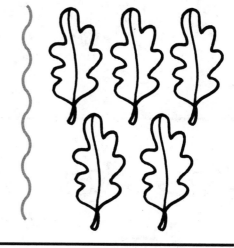

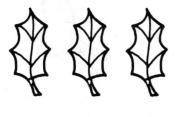

Name: _____

Compare the sets in each pair. Color the set that has **fewer**.

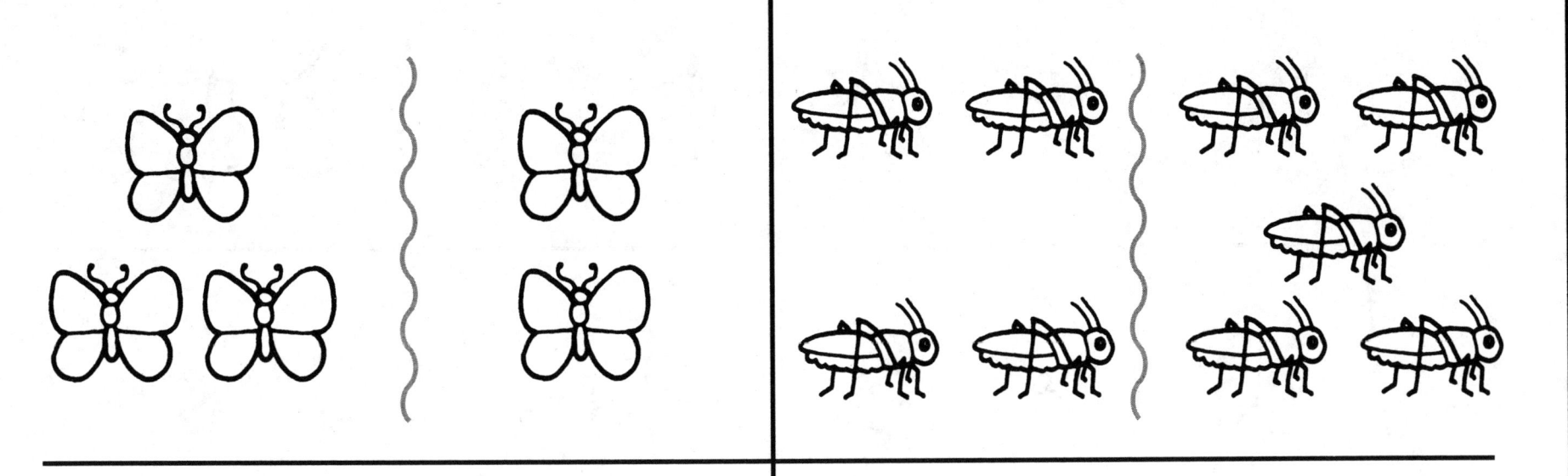

Name: _____

Match each number to its word.

1 •   • two

2 •   • one

3 •   • four

4 •   • three

5 •   • six

6 •   • seven

7 •   • five

8 •   • eight

 **100**

Name: _____

Match each number to its word.

9 •   • nine

10 •   • eleven

11 •   • twelve

12 •   • ten

13 •   • fourteen

14 •   • thirteen

15 •   • sixteen

16 •   • fifteen

Name: _____

Match each number to its word.

| 17 | • | • | twenty |

| 18 | • | • | nineteen |

| 19 | • | • | eighteen |

| 20 | • | • | seventeen |

| 21 | • | • | twenty-four |

| 22 | • | • | twenty-two |

| 23 | • | • | twenty-one |

| 24 | • | • | twenty-three |

Name: _____

Match each number to its word.

(30) •   • forty   (70) •   • eighty

(40) •   • fifty   (80) •   • seventy

(50) •   • sixty   (90) •   • one hundred

(60) •   • thirty   (100) •   • ninety

Write the missing numbers to complete the chart.

1									10
11									20
21									30
31									40
41									50

Name: _____

Write the missing numbers to complete the chart.

51									60
61									70
71									80
81									90
91									100

Trace the word.

red

red

red

Write **red**.

_____

- - - - - - - - - - - -

_____

Which things are **red** in real life? Color them.

 ☆106☆ Name: _____

Color: Red

Circle each **red**.

red   run   rot

bar   red   red

Draw a strawberry. Color each strawberry **red**.

Write **red**. _____

The strawberries are _____ .

Name: _____

Trace the word. ✏️

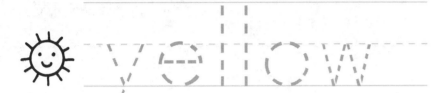

Write **yellow**.

_____

- - - - - - - - - - - - - - - - - - - -

Which things are **yellow** in real life? Color them.

Name: _____

Circle each **yellow**.

wall   yellow   your

yellow   anyhow   yellow

Draw a banana. Color each banana **yellow**.

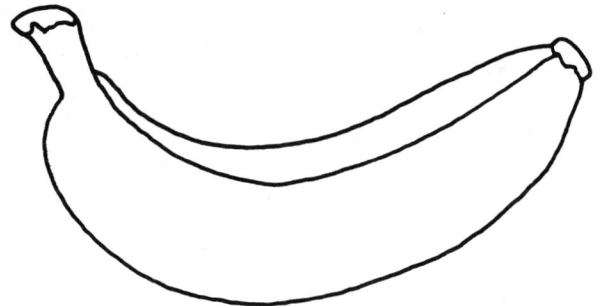

Write **yellow**.

I want to eat a _____ banana.

Name: _____

Trace the word.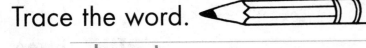

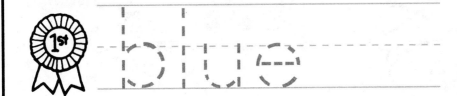

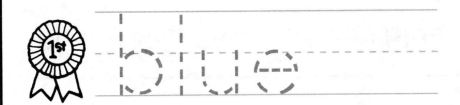

Write **blue**.

_____

- - - - - - - - - - - - -

_____

Which things are **blue** in real life?
Color them.

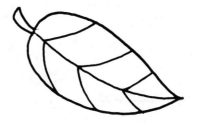

Name: _____

Circle each **blue**.

bulb   ball   blue

blue   blue   bold

Draw a bird. Color each bird **blue**.

Write **blue**. _____

Watch the _____ birds fly.

Trace the word.

green

green

green

Write **green**.

Which things are **green** in real life? Color them.

Name: _____

Circle each **green**.

great   green   green
green   seen   game

Draw a caterpillar. Color each caterpillar **green**.

Write **green**.

_____

The caterpillars are _____ .

Color the picture. Use the Color Key.

Color Key

= red

= green

= yellow

= blue

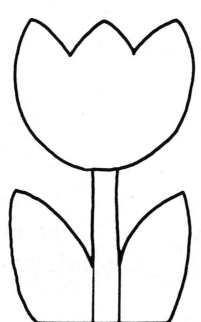

Name: _____

Write the color for each picture.
Use the words in the box.
Then color the pictures.

blue   green   yellow   red

_____

_____

_____

_____

Name: _____

Trace the word.

orange

orange

orange

Write **orange**.

_____

- - - - - - - - - - - - - - - -

_____

Which things are **orange** in real life? Color them.

Name: _____

Circle each **orange**.

orange   grain   orange

grand   orange   cover

Draw a pumpkin. Color each pumpkin **orange**.

Write **orange**.

_____

Look at the big _____ pumpkins.

Name: _____

Trace the word.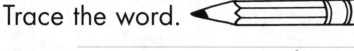

 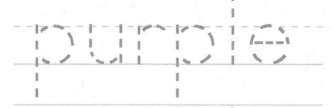

Write **purple**.

_____

- - - - - - - - - - - - - -

Which things are **purple** in real life? Color them.

 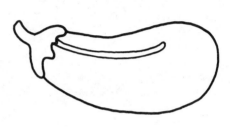

Name: _____

Circle each **purple**.

party   purple   play

quiet   purple   purple

Draw a bunch of grapes. Color the grapes **purple**.

Write **purple**.

_____

Let's eat the _____ grapes.

Trace the word.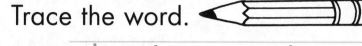

Write **black**.

_____

_____

Which things are **black** in real life? Color them.

Name: _____

Circle each **black**.

black	back	black
black	bend	ball

Draw a crow. Color each crow **black**.

Write **black**. _____

I see two _____ crows.

Trace the word.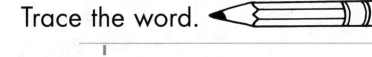

Write **brown**.

_____

_____

Which things are **brown** in real life? Color them.

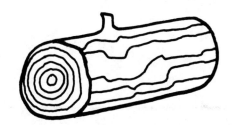

Name: _____

Circle each **brown**.

blow   brown   clown

brown   bring   brown

Draw a bear. Color each bear **brown**.

Write **brown**.

_____

The two big bears are _____ .

Name: _____

Color the picture. Use the Color Key.

Color Key

◯ = purple   🎈 = orange

🐻 = brown   🎩 = black

Name: _____

Write the color for each picture.
Use the words in the box.
Then color the pictures.

purple   black   brown   orange

_____

_____

_____

_____

Color the picture. Use the Color Key.

Color Key

 red

 blue

 yellow

 green

 orange

 purple

 black

 brown

Name: _____

Color the picture. Use the Color Key.

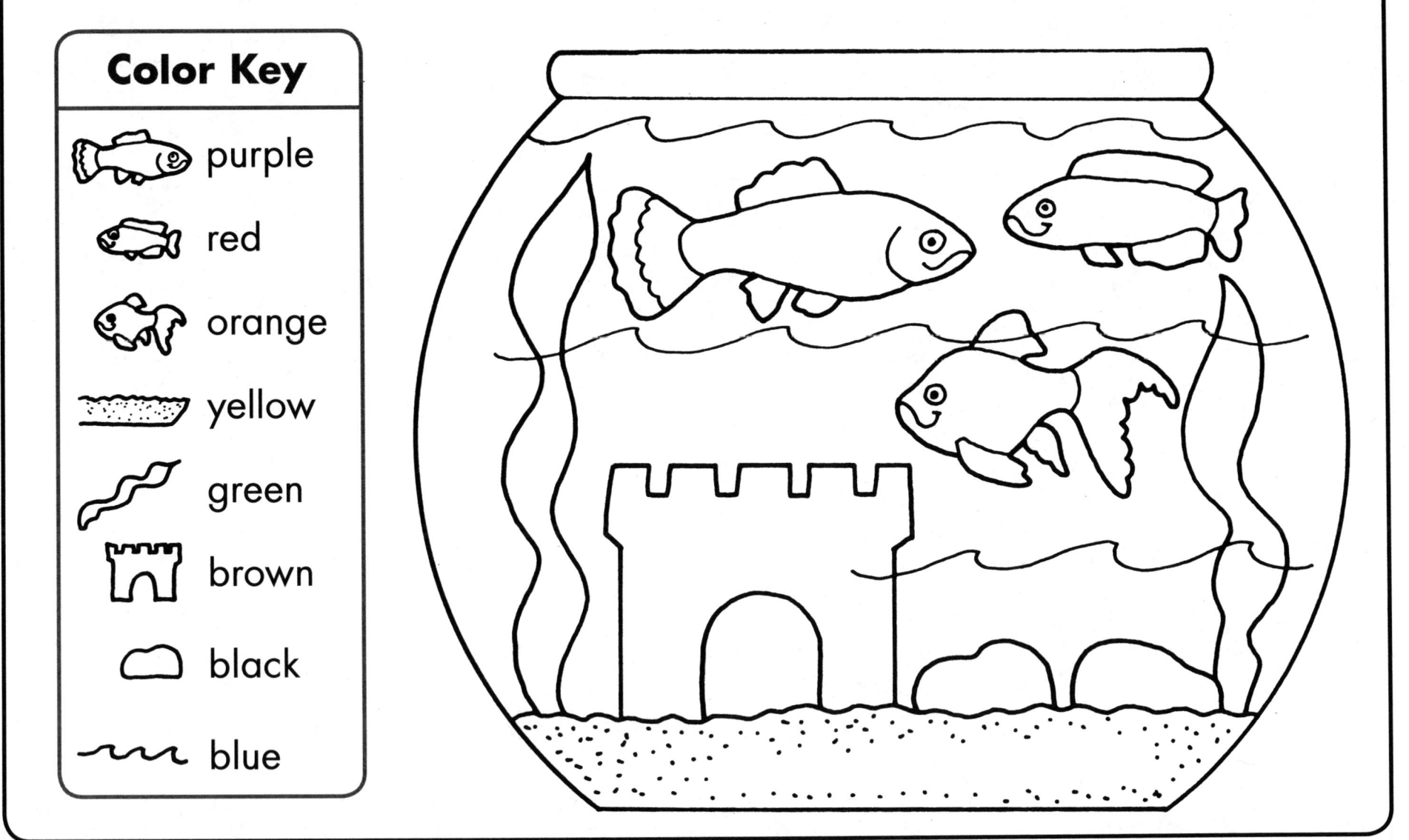

Color Key

- purple
- red
- orange
- yellow
- green
- brown
- black
- blue

Name: _____

Make a color pattern
in each row.
Use the Color Key.

Color Key

 = red   = blue   = yellow

1.

2.

3.

 **128**

Name: _____

Color Patterns: AB

Make a color pattern in each row.
Use the Color Key.

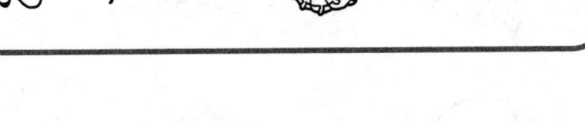

Color Key

 = red   = yellow   = green

1.

2.

3.

Make a color pattern
in each row.
Use the Color Key.

like you you Do I (handwritten)

Color Key

 = purple   = orange   = brown

1.

2.

3.

 130 Name: _____

Make a color pattern
in each row.
Use the Color Key.

Color Key

 = purple    = black   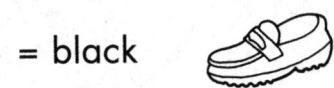 = brown

1.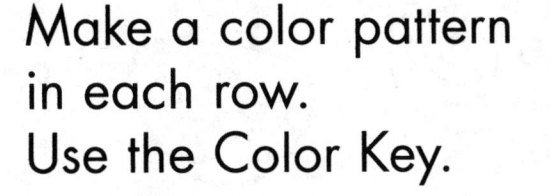

2.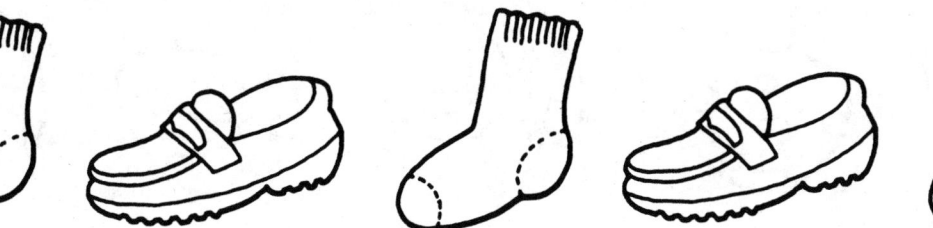

3.

Make a color pattern
in each row.
Use the Color Key.

Color Key

= red   = orange   = blue

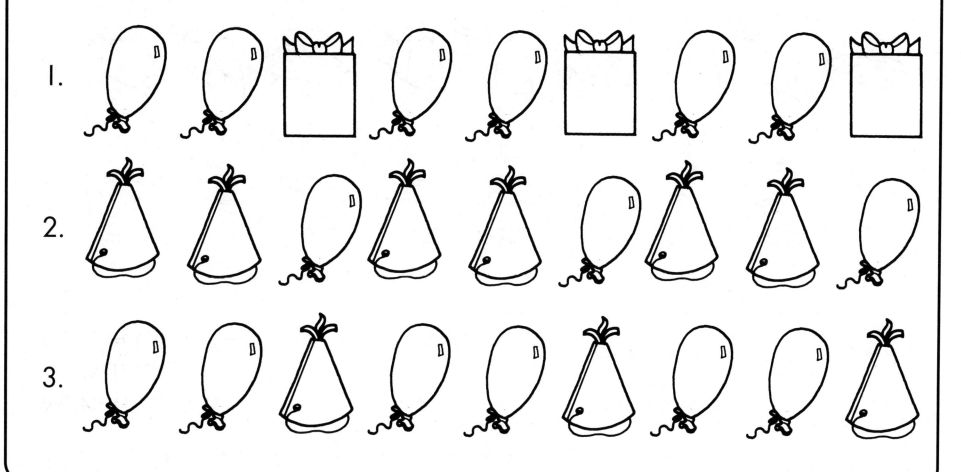

1.

2.

3.

Name: _____

Make a color pattern
in each row.
Use the Color Key.

Color Key		

= brown   = green   = purple

1.

2.

3.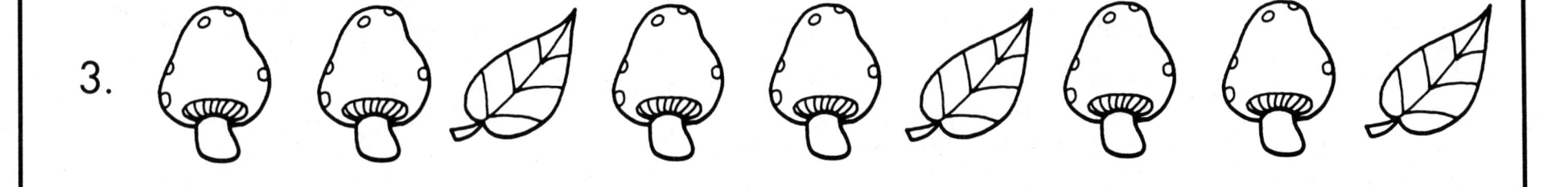

Make a color pattern
in each row.
Use the Color Key.

Color Key

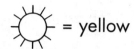 = yellow   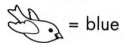 = blue   = green

1.

2.

3.

4.

 Name: _____

Make a color pattern in each row.
Use the Color Key.

Color Key		
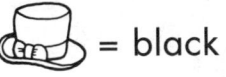 = black	 = red	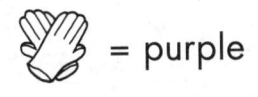 = purple

1.

2.

3.

4.

Name: _____

Make a color pattern
in each row.
Use the Color Key.

Color Key		
= green	= red	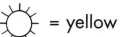 = yellow

1.

2.

3.

4.

 136

Name: _____

Color Patterns: AABB

Make a color pattern
in each row.
Use the Color Key.

Color Key

 = blue    = orange   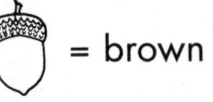 = brown

1.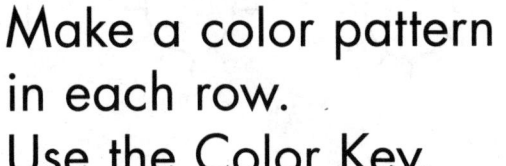

2.

3.

4.

Now I Know My Numbers, Colors, Shapes & More © 2014 Scholastic Teaching Resources • page 152

Name: _____

Make a color pattern
in each row.
Use the Color Key.

Color Key

 = purple   = brown   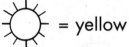 = yellow

1.

2.

3.

4.

Name: _____

Make a color pattern
in each row.
Use the Color Key.

Color Key

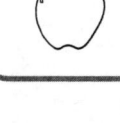 = red    = orange    = yellow

1.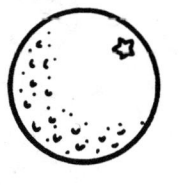

2.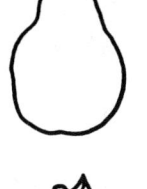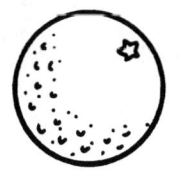

3.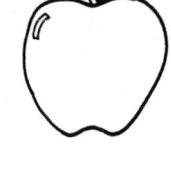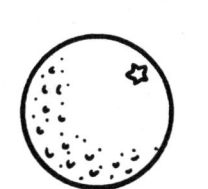

4.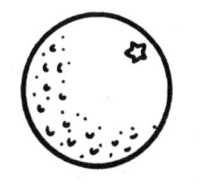

Trace each **circle**.

Color each **circle**.

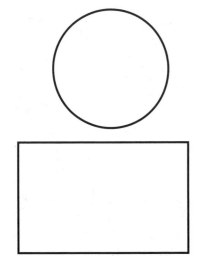

140

Name: _____

Trace the word.

☺ circle

☺ circle

☺ circle

Write **circle**.

_____

_____

Trace each **circle**.

Draw a ◯ for a ball.

Trace each **square**.

Color each **square**.

Name: _____

Trace the word.

square

square

square

Write **square**.

_____

_____

Trace each **square**.

Draw a ☐ for a window.

Name: _____

Trace each **triangle**.

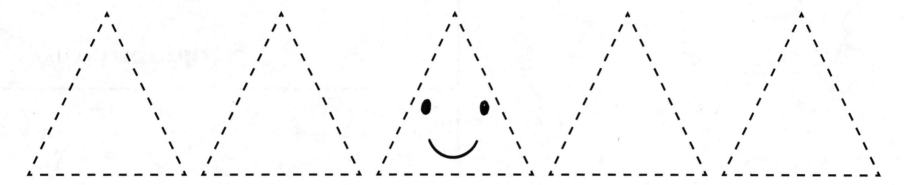

Color each **triangle**.

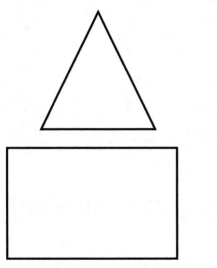
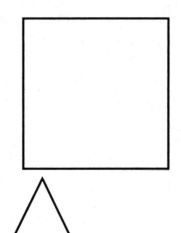

Name: _____

Trace the word.

triangle

triangle

triangle

Write **triangle**.

_____

_____

Trace each **triangle**.

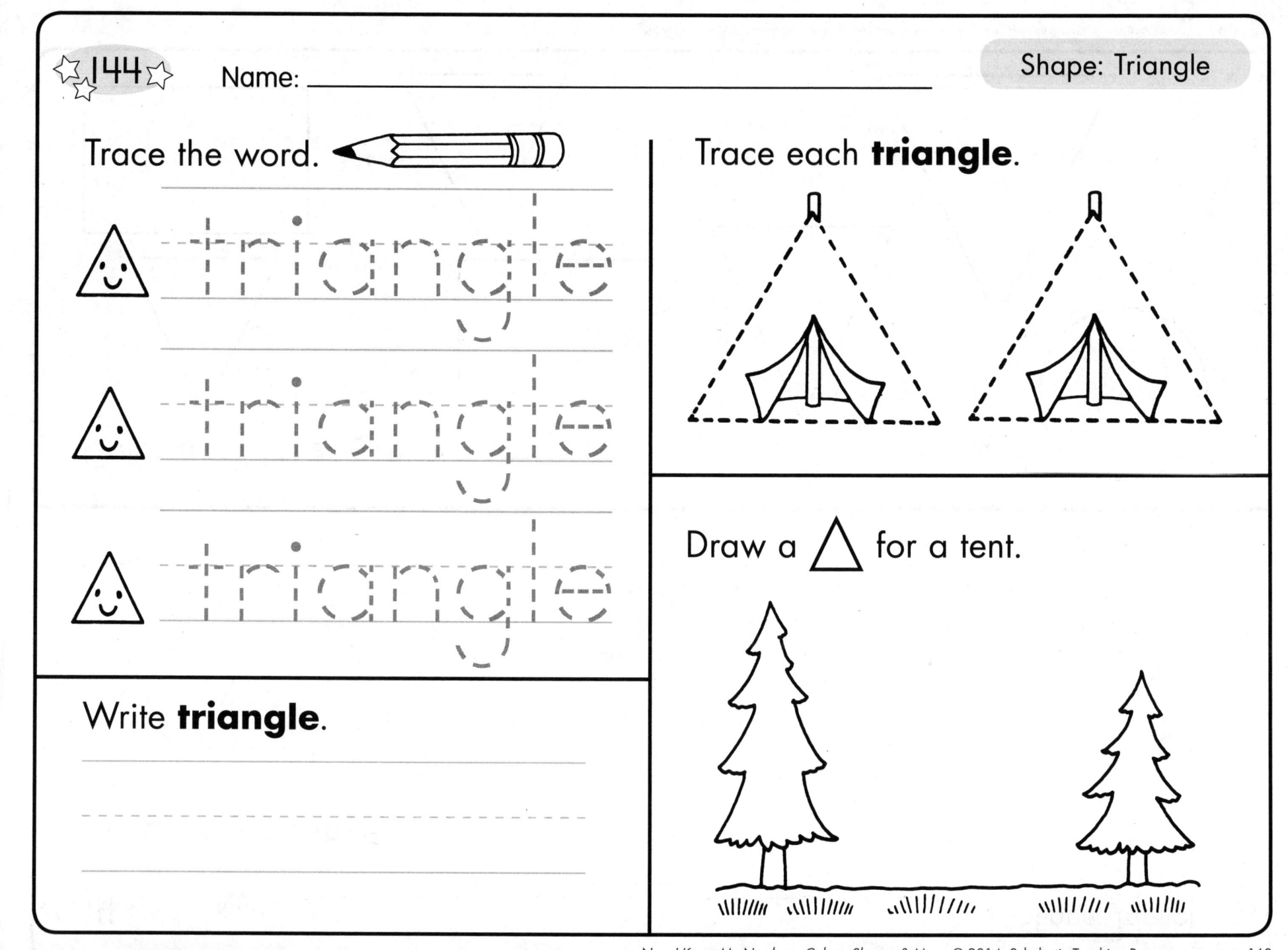

Draw a △ for a tent.

Name: _____

Trace each **rectangle**.

Color each **rectangle**.

Name: _____

Trace the word.

rectangle

rectangle

rectangle

Write **rectangle**.

_____

_____

Trace each **rectangle**.

Draw a ☐ for a gift.

Name: _____

Color the picture. Use the Color Key.

Color Key

○ green

□ red

△ blue

▭ brown

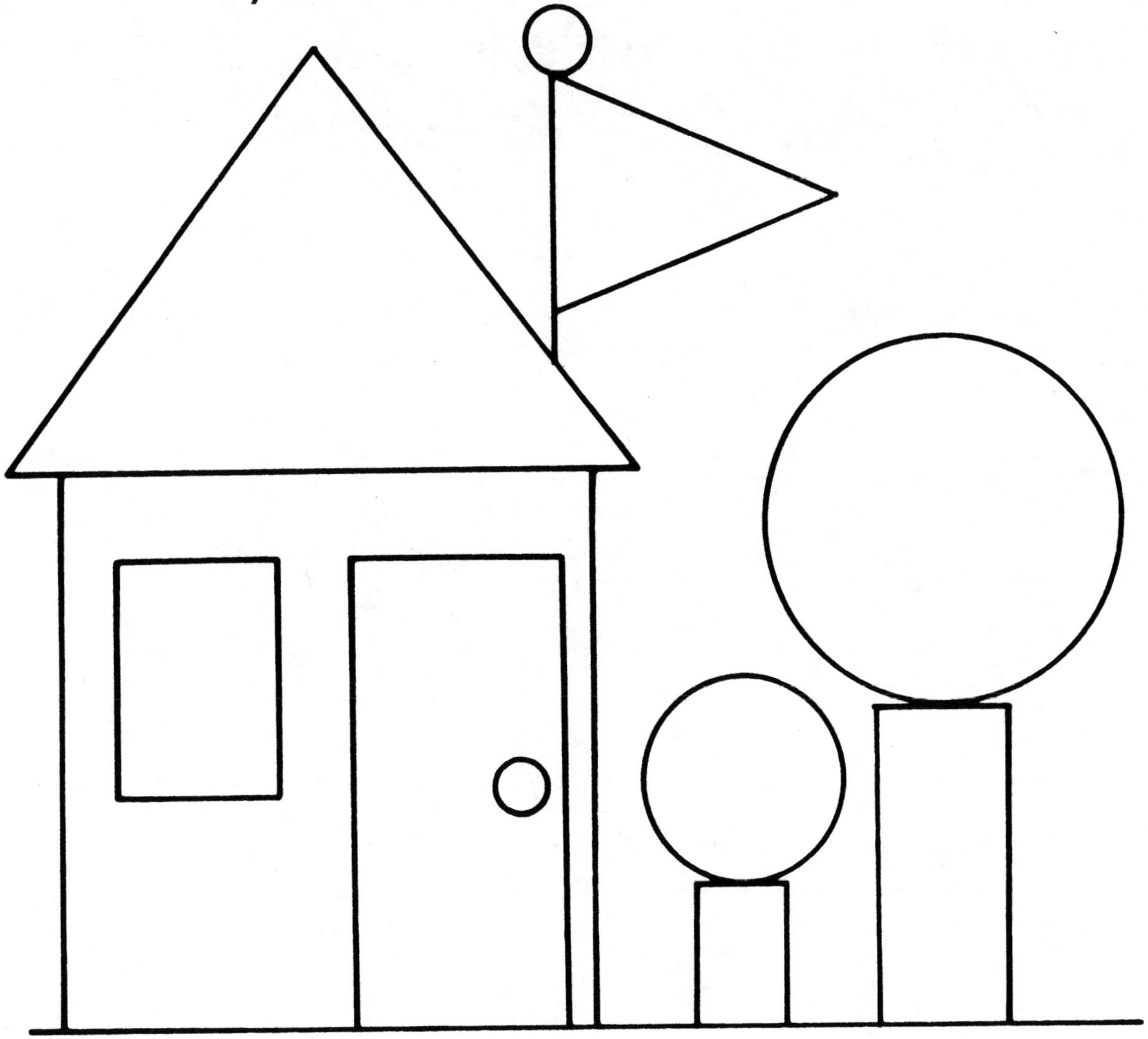

Name: _____

Write the name for each shape.
Use the words in the box.

| square   circle   rectangle   triangle |

_____

_ _ _ _ _ _ _ _ _ _ _ _ _ _ _ _

_____

_ _ _ _ _ _ _ _ _ _ _ _ _ _ _ _

Name: _____

Trace each **oval**.

Color each **oval**.

Name: _____

Trace the word.

oval

oval

oval

Write **oval**.

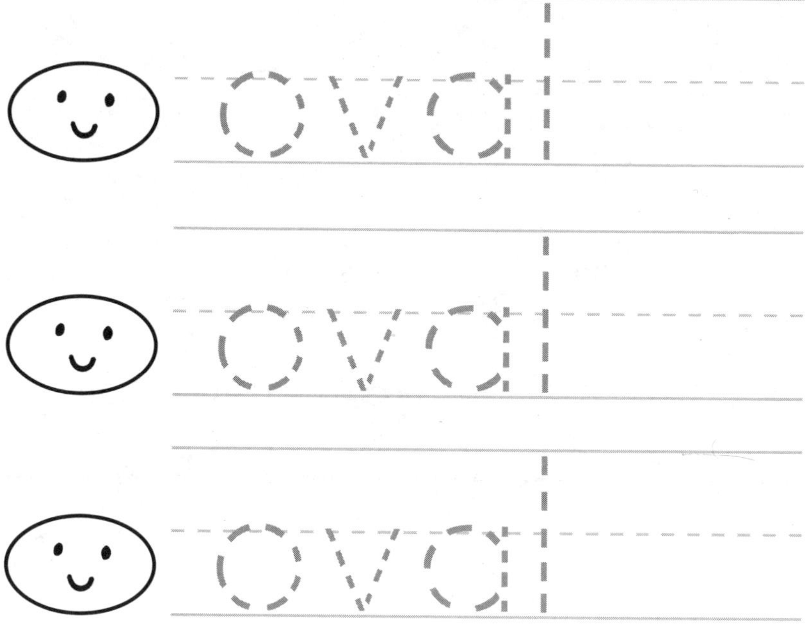

Trace each **oval**.

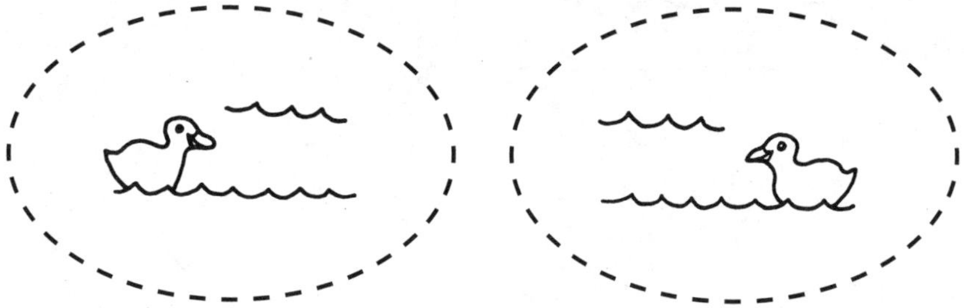

Draw an 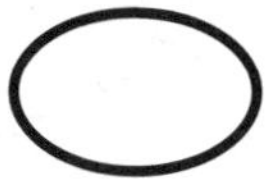 ⬭ for a pond.

Name: _____

Trace each **octagon**.

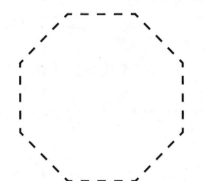 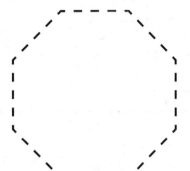  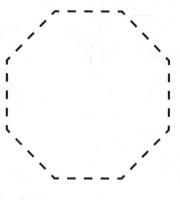

Color each **octagon**.

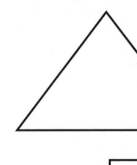 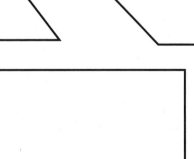  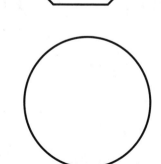

Name: _____

Trace the word.

octagon

octagon

octagon

Write **octagon**.

_____

_____

Trace each **octagon**.

STOP   STOP

Draw a ⬡ as a sign on the post.

Name: _____

Trace each **star**.

Color each **star**.

   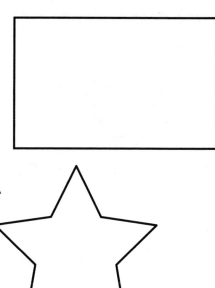

Name: _____

Trace the word.

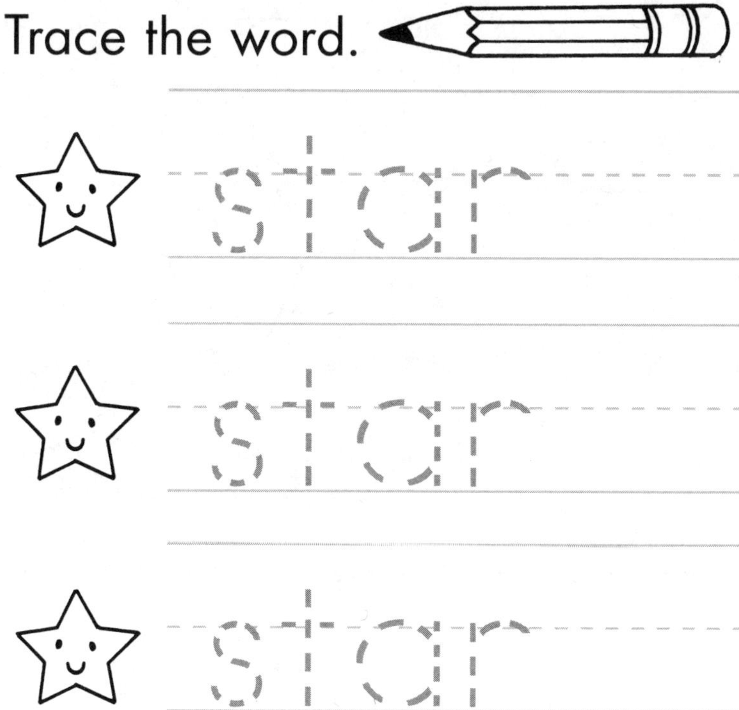

star

star

star

Write **star**.

_____

_____

Trace each **star**.

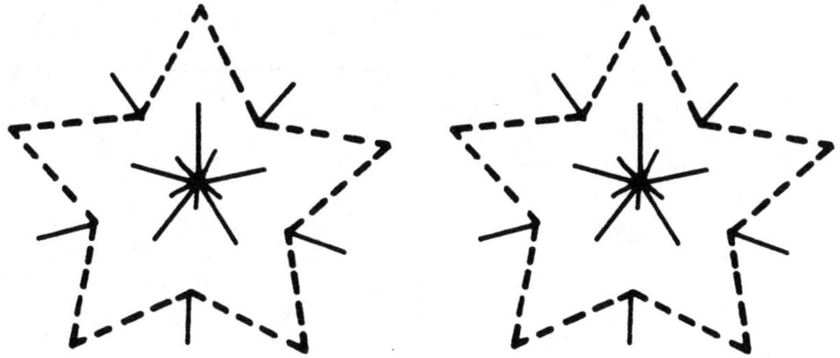

Draw a ☆ in the sky.

Name: _____

Trace each **diamond**.

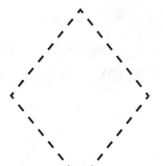 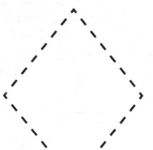  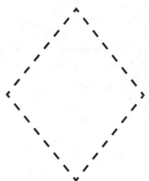 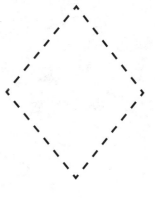

Color each **diamond**.

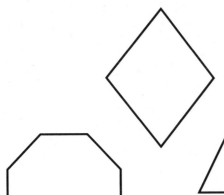   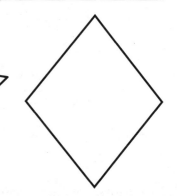

Name: _____

Trace the word.

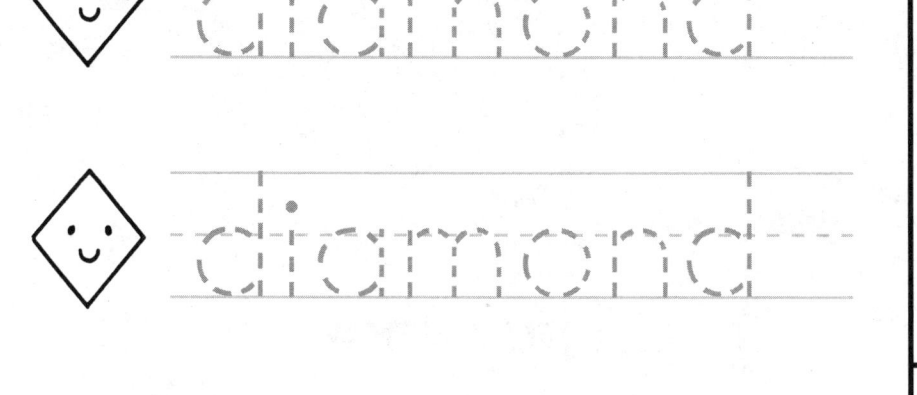

diamond

diamond

diamond

Write **diamond**.

_____

_____

Trace each **diamond**.

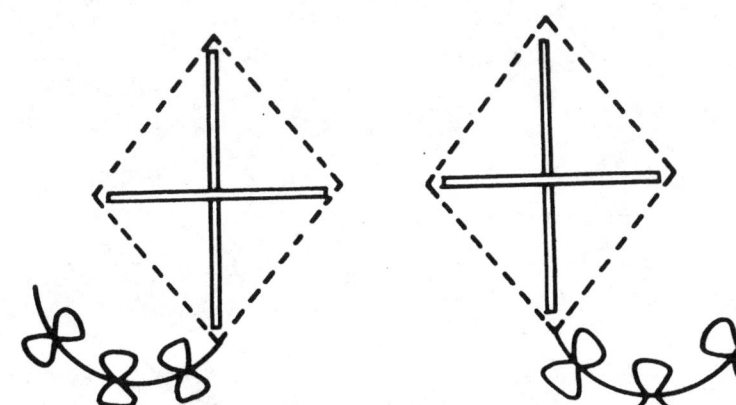

Draw a ◇ for a kite.

Color the picture. Use the Color Key.

Color Key

⬭ blue

⬡ red

☆ yellow

◇ green

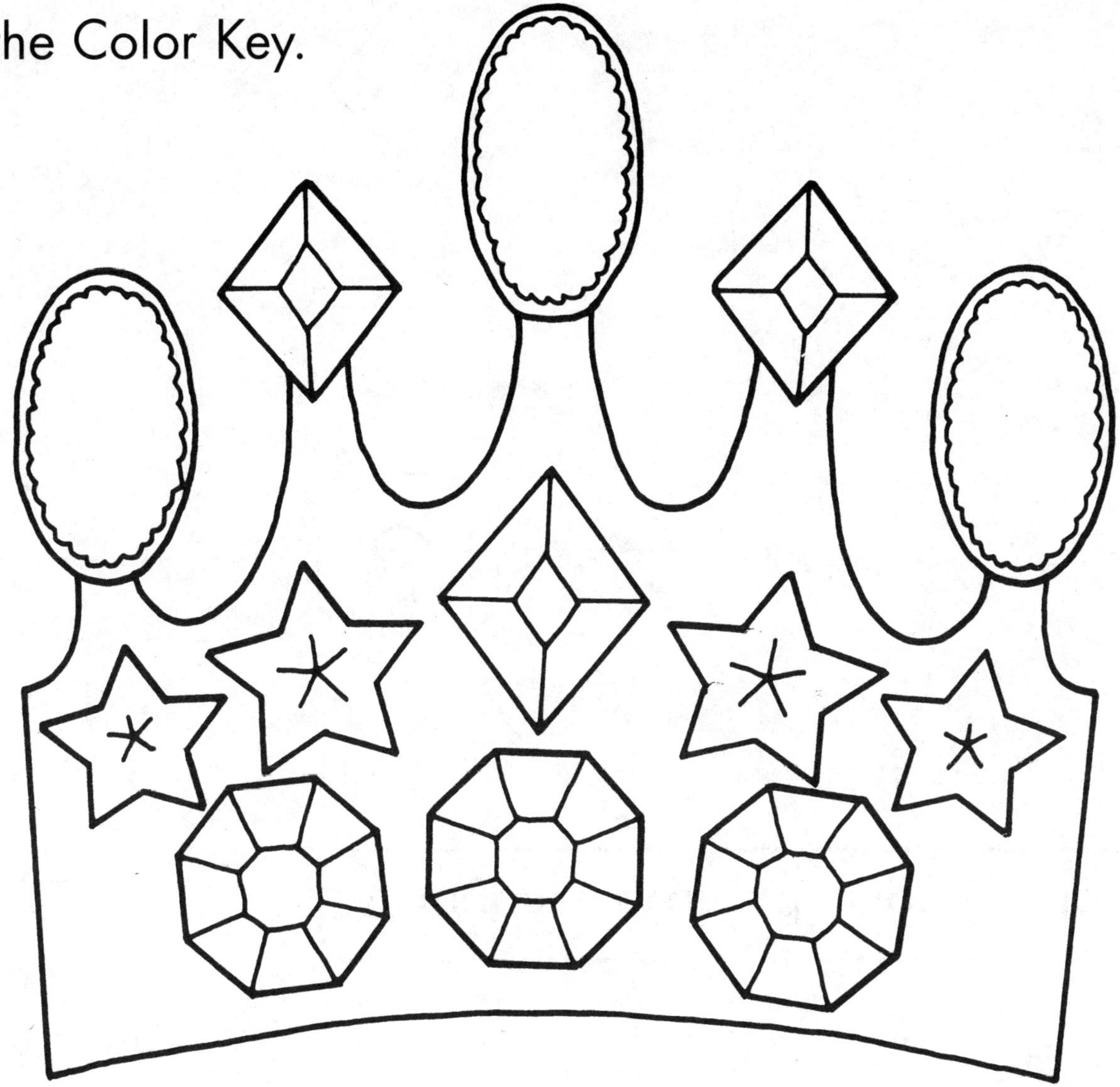

Write the name for each shape.
Use the words in the box.

octagon   oval   diamond   star

_____

_____

_____

_____

Name: _____

Draw shapes to complete each pattern.

1.    _____ _____

2.    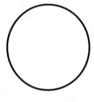 _____ _____

3.   _____ _____

Name: _____

Draw shapes to complete each pattern.

1. 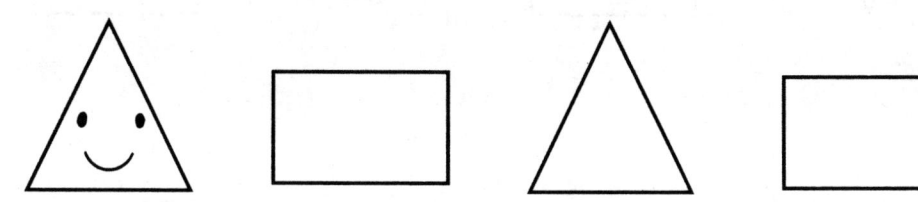 _____ _____

2. 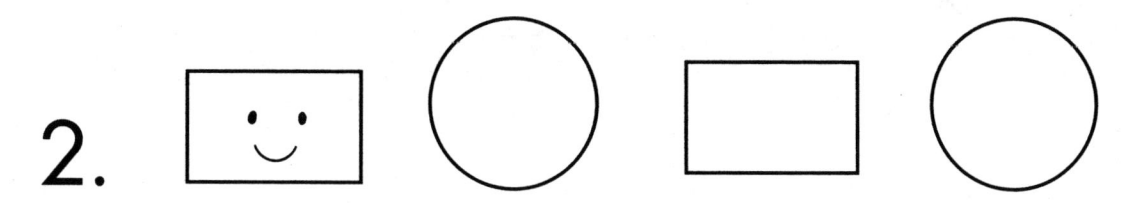 _____ _____

3. 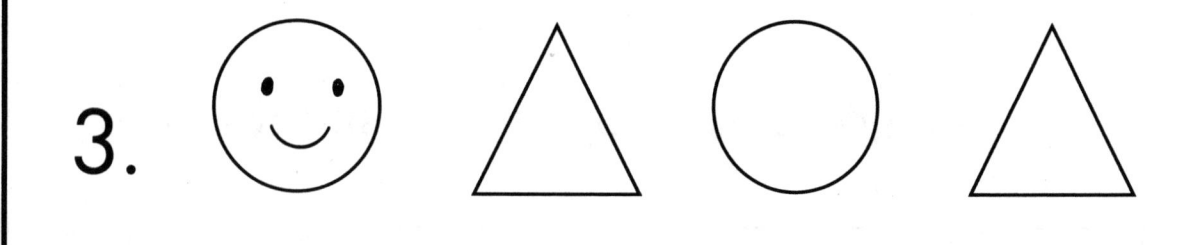 _____ _____

Draw shapes to complete each pattern.

1.   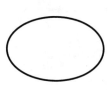 _____ _____

2.  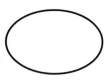 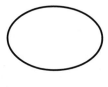 _____ _____

3.   _____ _____

 **162**

Name: _____

Draw shapes to complete each pattern.

1.   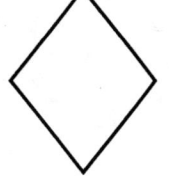  _____ _____

2.   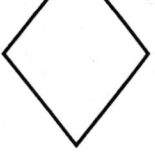  _____ _____

3.  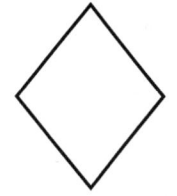  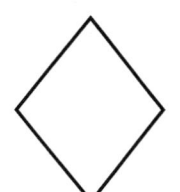 _____ _____

Draw shapes to complete each pattern.

1. 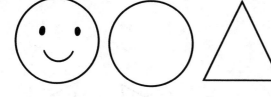 _____ _____ _____

2. 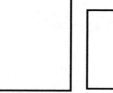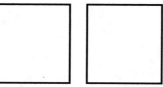 _____ _____ _____

3. 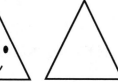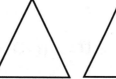 _____ _____ _____

Name: _____

Draw shapes to complete each pattern.

1. ◇ ◇ ◯ ◇ ◇ ___ ___ ___

2. ☆ ☆ ⬡ ☆ ☆ ___ ___ ___

3. ◯ ◯ ◇ ◯ ◯ ___ ___ ___

Draw shapes to complete each pattern.

1.  _____ _____ _____

2.   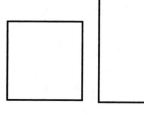 _____ _____ _____

3. 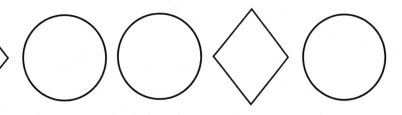 _____ _____ _____

Draw shapes to complete each pattern.

1. 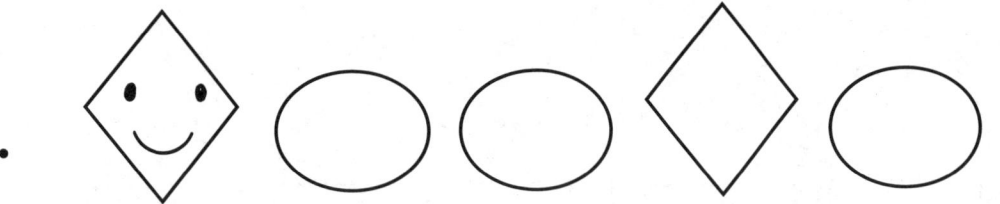 ___ ___ ___

2. 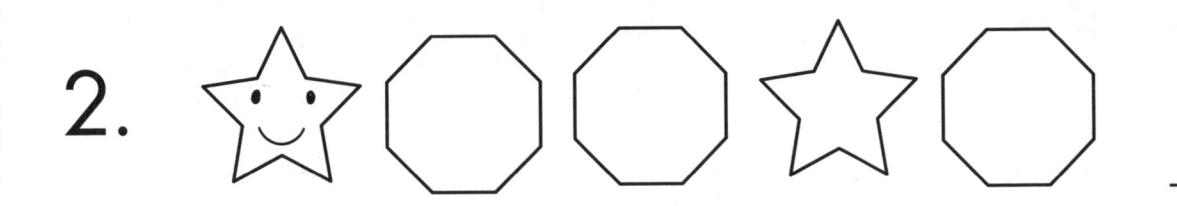 ___ ___ ___

3. ___ ___ ___

Draw shapes to complete each pattern.

1.   _____ _____ _____ _____

2.   _____ _____ _____

3.   _____ _____ _____ _____

Name: _____

Draw shapes to complete each pattern.

1. ☆ ☆ ◯ ◯ ___ ___ ___ ___

2. ▯ ▯ ⬡ ⬡ ___ ___ ___ ___

3. ◇ ◇ ☆ ☆ ___ ___ ___ ___

Draw shapes to complete each pattern.

1.  ___ ___ ___ ___

2.  ___ ___ ___ ___

3.  ___ ___ ___ ___

Name: _____

Draw shapes to complete each pattern.

1.  _____ _____ _____

2. _____ _____ _____

3. _____ _____ _____

Name: _____

Color each shape.
Draw an x on the
blue △.

Color each shape.
Draw an x on the
red ○.

blue

yellow

orange

purple

red

green

red

black

Name: _____

Color each shape.
Draw an x on the
orange ☐.

brown

green

blue

orange

Color each shape.
Draw an x on the
green ☆.

blue

black

green

red

☆173☆ Name: _____

Color each shape.
Draw an x on the
small blue △.

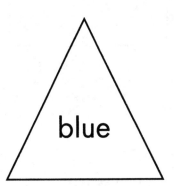

blue

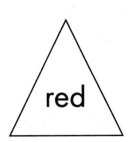

red

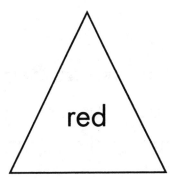

red

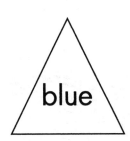

blue

Color each shape.
Draw an x on the
big red ○.

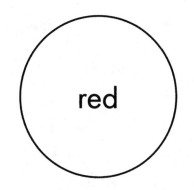

red

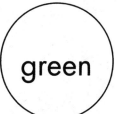

green

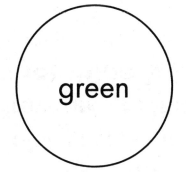

green

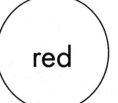

red

Name: _____

Color each shape.
Draw an x on the
big orange ☐.

yellow

orange

yellow

orange

Color each shape.
Draw an x on the
small blue ☆.

red

red

blue

blue

Color each shape brown.
Draw an x on the
small ◇.

Color each shape red.
Draw an x on the
big ☆.

Name: _____

Color each shape green.
Draw an x on the
big ⬡.

Color each shape purple.
Draw an x on the
small ▭.

Name: _____

Draw pictures to complete each pattern.

1.    _____ _____

2.    _____ _____

3.   _____ _____

Name: _____

Draw pictures to complete each pattern.

1.      _____ _____

2.         _____ _____

3.     _____ _____

Draw pictures to complete each pattern.

1.  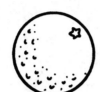   _____ _____

2.    _____ _____

3.   _____ _____

Name: _____

Draw pictures to complete each pattern.

1.   _____ _____ _____ _____

2.    _____ _____ _____

3.    _____ _____

Name: _____

Write letters to complete each pattern.

1.  D  E  D  E 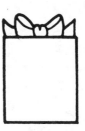 D 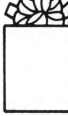 E

2.  H I H  I

3.  L  M  L  M

☆182☆ Name: _____

Write letters to complete each pattern.

1.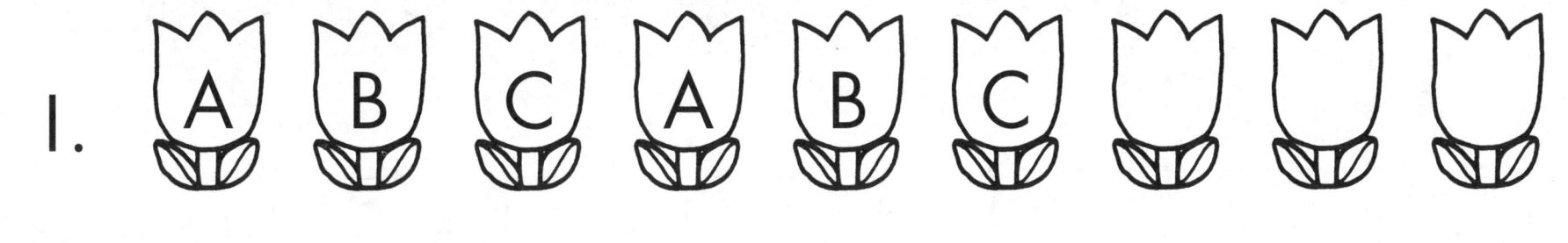

2.

3.

Name: _____

Write letters to complete each pattern.

1.

O   P   P   O   P   P

2.

S   S   T   S   S   T

3.

X   Y   Z   X

Patterns: Letters

Name: _____

☆184☆

Write letters to complete each pattern.

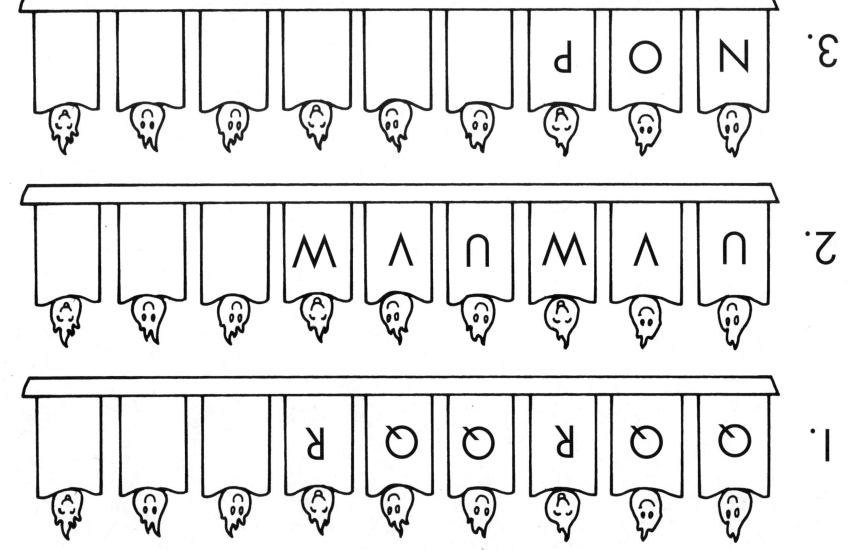

1. Q O R Q O R Q O __ __

2. U V W U V W U V __ __

3. N O P N O P __ __ __

Name: _____

Write letters to complete each pattern.

1.

b c b c b c

2.

i j i j

3.

m n m n

Name: _____

Write letters to complete each pattern.

1.

2.

3.

Name: _____

Write letters to complete each pattern.

1.

2.

3.

Name: _____

Write letters to complete each pattern.

1. p p q p p q

2. s t u s t u

3. w x x

Name: _____

Write letters to complete each pattern.

1.

A b A b

2.

p D B

3.

G c c

Name: _____

Write letters to complete each pattern.

1.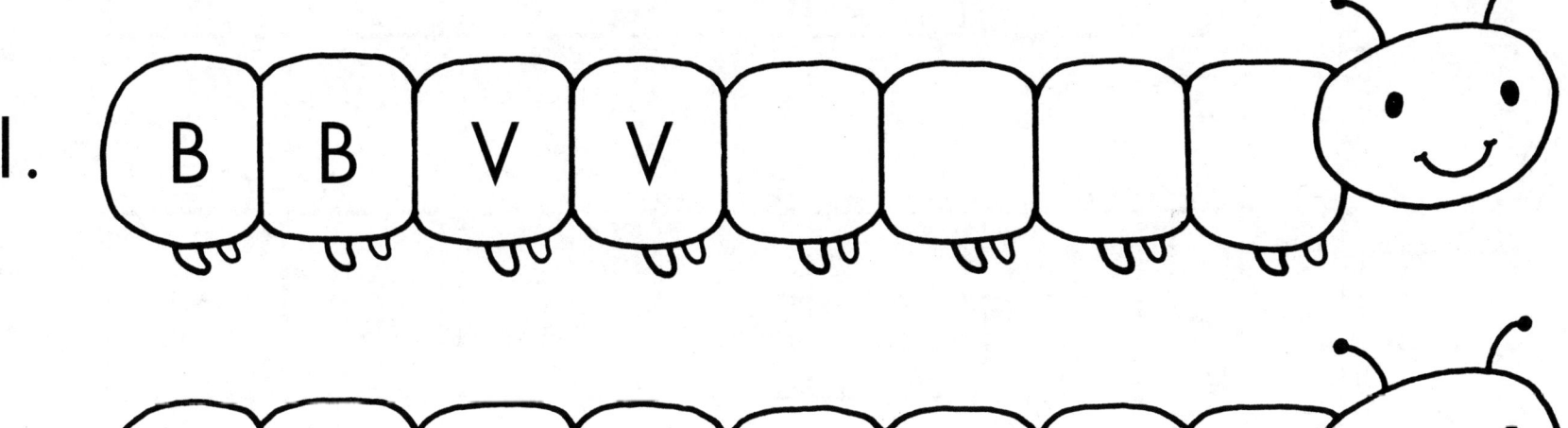

B B V V

2.

m O m O

3.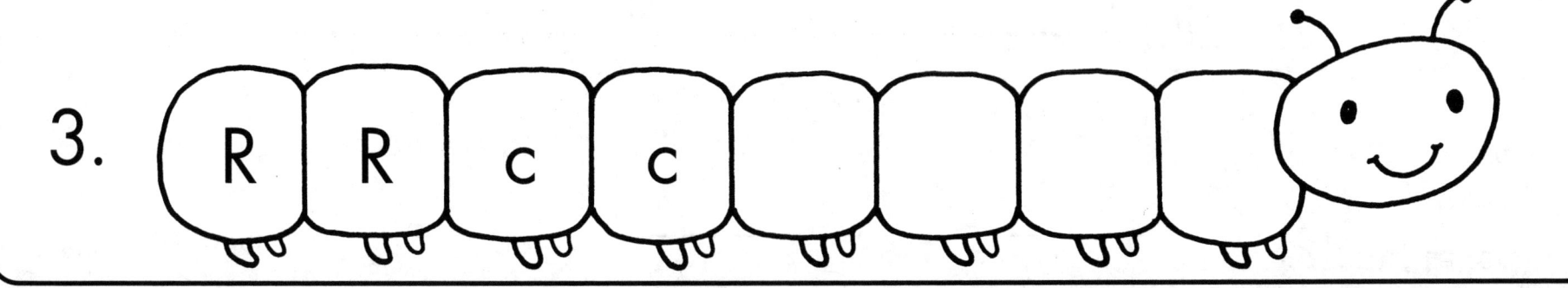

R R c c

Name: _____

Write numbers to complete each pattern.

1.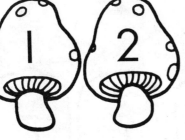

2.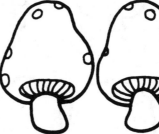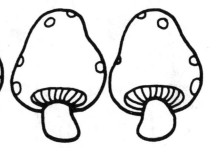

3.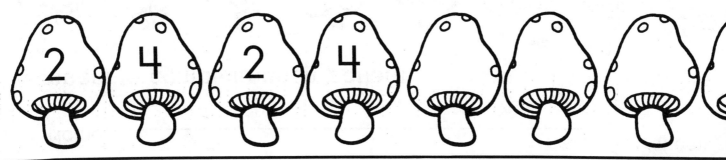

Name: _____

Write numbers to complete each pattern.

1. 1 3 1 3

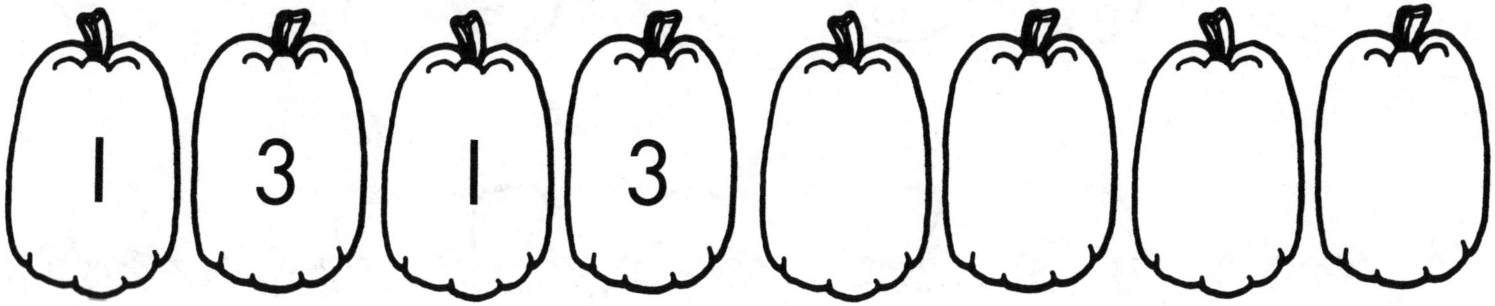

2. 2 2 4 4

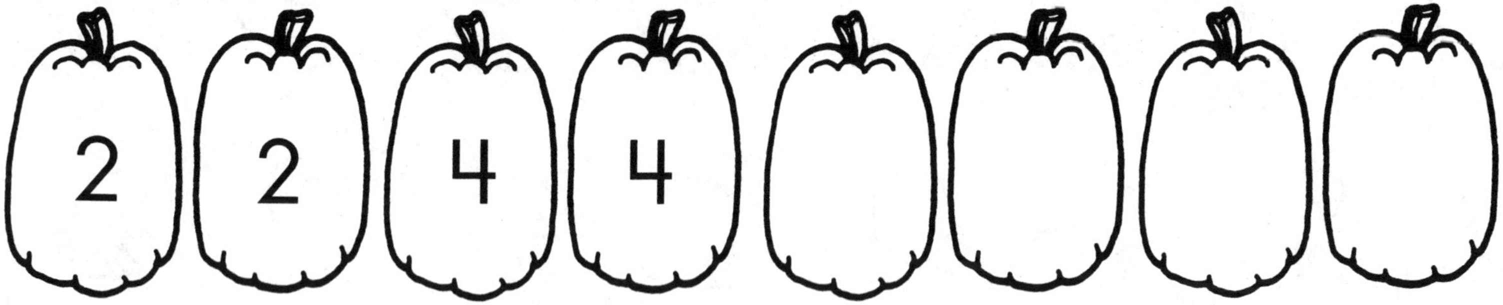

3. 3 3 5 5

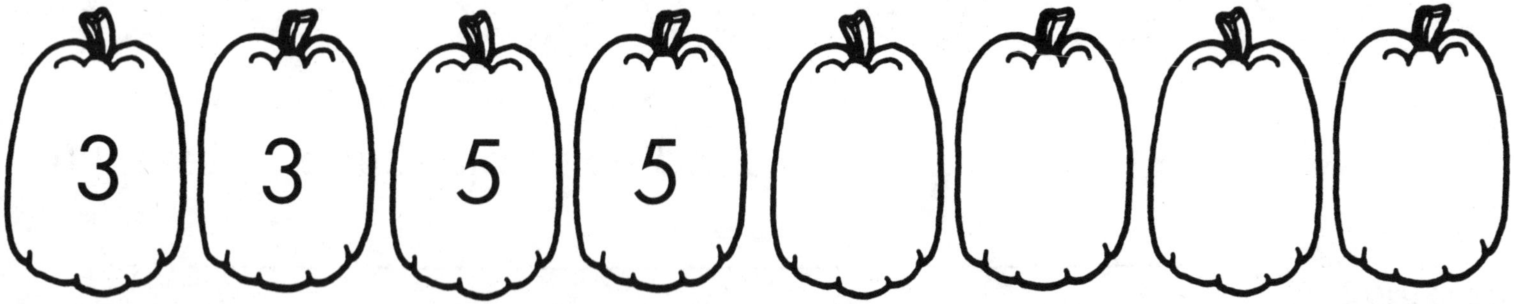

Write numbers to complete each pattern.

1.

8   8   9   8   8   9

2.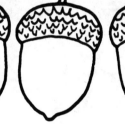

6   1   3   6   1   3

3.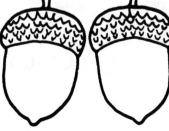

9   4   4

Name: _____

Write numbers to complete each pattern.

1. 6 6 8 8

2. 7 9 7 9

3. 5 5 2 2

Complete each pattern.

1. | 2 | A | B | 2 | A | B | | | |

2. | T | 5 | V | | | | | | |

3. | 4 | S | S | | | | | | |

Name: _____

Complete each pattern.

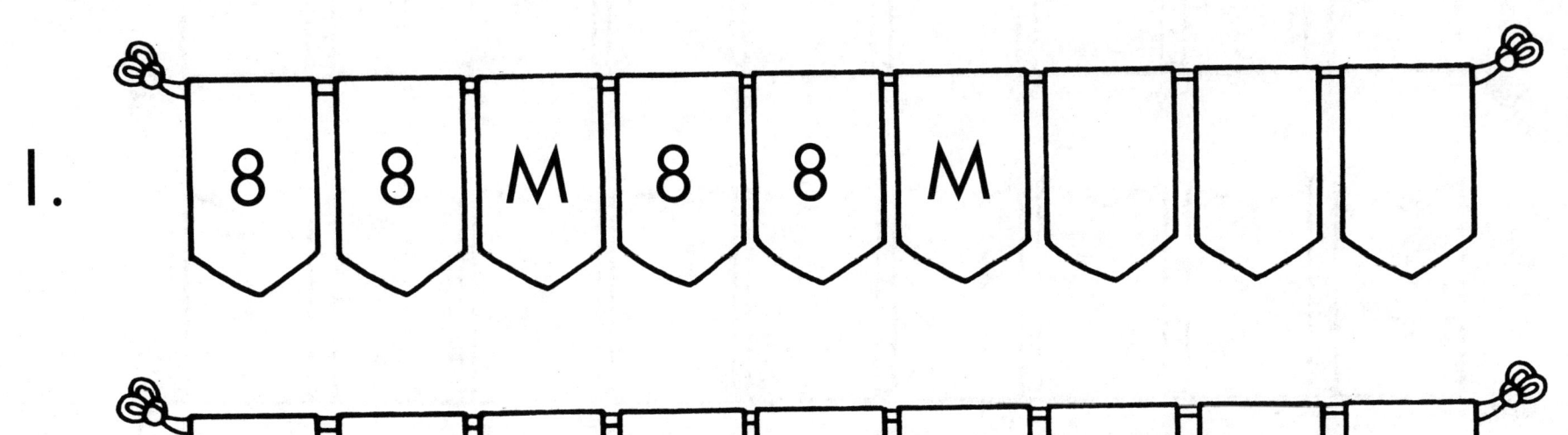

1. 8 8 M 8 8 M

2. F F 9

3. 3 D C

Name: _____

What comes next in each pattern? Circle your answer.

1.  |

2.  |

3. |

Draw your own pattern! Use two pictures.

___ ___ ___ ___ ___ ___

198 Name: _____

What comes next in each pattern? Circle your answer.

1.

2.

3.

Draw your own pattern! Use three shapes.

Name: _____

Finish labeling each pattern.

1. A   B   A   B   A   B   ___   ___

2. A   B   A   B   ___   ___   ___   ___

Draw your own **AB** pattern. Use pictures.

___   ___   ___   ___   ___   ___
A   B   A   B   A   B

⭐200⭐ Name: _____

Finish labeling each pattern.

○ □ ○ □ ○ □ ○ □

1. A   B   A   B   __   __   __   __

△ ☆ △ ☆ △ ☆ △ ☆

2. A   B   __   __   __   __   __   __

Draw your own **AB** pattern. Label the pattern.

___ ___ ___ ___ ___ ___

Finish labeling each pattern.

1. <u>A</u> <u>A</u> <u>B</u> <u>A</u> <u>A</u> <u>B</u> <u> </u> <u> </u> <u> </u>

2. <u>A</u> <u>A</u> <u>B</u> <u> </u> <u> </u> <u> </u> <u> </u> <u> </u> <u> </u>

Draw your own **AAB** pattern. Use pictures.

<u>   </u>   <u>   </u>   <u>   </u>   <u>   </u>   <u>   </u>   <u>   </u>

  A   A   B   A   A   B

Name: _____

Finish labeling each pattern.

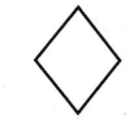  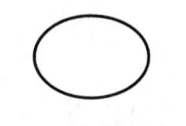 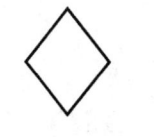 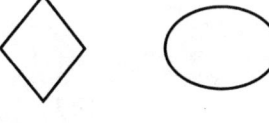 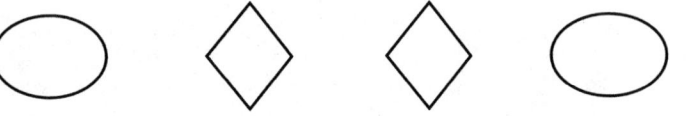

1. _A_ _A_ _B_ _A_ ___ ___ ___ ___ ___

  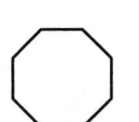 

2. _A_ _A_ _B_ ___ ___ ___ ___ ___ ___

Draw your own **AAB** pattern. Label the pattern.

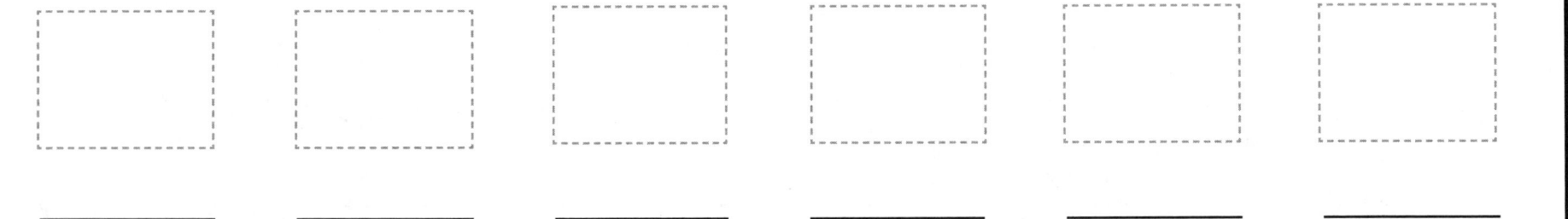

___ ___ ___ ___ ___ ___

Finish labeling each pattern.

1. A   B   B   A   B   B   ___   ___   ___

2. A   B   B   ___   ___   ___   ___   ___   ___

Draw your own **ABB** pattern. Use pictures.

___   ___   ___   ___   ___   ___

A   B   B   A   B   B

Name: _____

Finish labeling each pattern.

1. A   B   B   A   ___ ___ ___ ___ ___

2. A   B   B   ___ ___ ___ ___ ___ ___

Draw your own **ABB** pattern. Label the pattern.

___   ___   ___   ___   ___   ___

☆205☆ Name: _____

Finish labeling each pattern.

1. <u>A</u> <u>A</u> <u>B</u> <u>B</u> <u>A</u> <u>A</u> <u> </u> <u> </u>

2. <u>A</u> <u>A</u> <u>B</u> <u>B</u> <u> </u> <u> </u> <u> </u> <u> </u>

Draw your own **AABB** pattern. Use pictures.

<u> </u> <u> </u> <u> </u> <u> </u> <u> </u> <u> </u> <u> </u> <u> </u>
 A   A   B   B   A   A   B   B

Finish labeling each pattern.

1. A A B __ __ __ __ __

2. A A __ __ __ __ __ __

Draw your own **AABB** pattern. Label the pattern.

Name: _____

Finish labeling each pattern.

1. A   B   C   A   B   C   ___   ___   ___

2. A   B   C   ___   ___   ___   ___   ___   ___

Draw your own **ABC** pattern. Use pictures.

___   ___   ___   ___   ___   ___
A   B   C   A   B   C

Name: _____

Finish labeling each pattern.

1. A B C A ___ ___ ___ ___ ___

2. A B C ___ ___ ___ ___ ___ ___

Draw your own **ABC** pattern. Label the pattern.

___ ___ ___ ___ ___ ___